The Vital Questions Series

CLEAR THINKING FOR FAITHFUL LIVING

□ □

These books investigate key issues that make a practical difference in how Christians think and act. The goal is to provide a substantial, accessible discussion of issues about which Christians need to know more. This series is intended as a service to the church and to individuals with the aim of better preparing a "Christian mind," resulting in more faithful living.

Daniel Taylor, General Editor

Is God Intolerant?

Christian Thinking about the Call for Tolerance

□ □ □ □ □ □ □ □ □ □ □ □ □ DANIEL TAYLOR,

AUTHOR AND GENERAL EDITOR

Tyndale House Publishers, Inc., Wheaton, Illinois

For Edward E. Ericson—who started me thinking.

Visit Tyndale's exciting Web site at www.tyndale.com

Is God Intolerant? Christian Thinking about the Call for Tolerance

Copyright © 2003 by Daniel Taylor. All rights reserved.

Designed by Kelly Bennema with Luke Daab

Edited by Daniel Taylor and MaryLynn Layman

Scripture quotations are taken from the *Holy Bible,* New Living Translation, copyright © 1996, 2002. Used by permission of Tyndale House Publishers, Inc., Wheaton, Illinois 60189. All rights reserved.

Library of Congress Cataloging-in-Publication Data

Taylor, Daniel, date.
  Is God intolerant? : the clash of values over tolerance / Daniel Taylor.
    p. cm. — (Vital questions)
Includes bibliographical references and index.
  ISBN 0-8423-5439-5 (hc)
  1. Toleration. 2. Christian ethics. I. Title. II. Series: Vital questions (Tyndale House Publishers)
BJ1275. T39 2003
241'.4—dc21   2002151259

Printed in the United States of America

07   06   05   04   03
7   6   5   4   3   2   1

Contents

Acknowledgments...*vii*
Introduction...*1*

1 A Short History of
   the Idea of Tolerance 9

2 What *Is* Tolerance?
   Definitions and Distinctions 17

3 The Use and Misuse of
   Tolerance in the Culture Wars 47

4 Tolerance and the Bible:
   How Tolerant Is God? 77

5 Practical Suggestions,
   Guidelines, and Principles 109

   Discussion Questions 122

Notes...*129*
Recommended Reading.................................*131*
Topical Index *132*
About the Author..*134*

Acknowledgments

I would like to thank John Wilson and Mickey Maudlin for their enthusiasm for an article on tolerance in *Christianity Today* that was the impetus for this longer exploration. Thanks also to my colleague Daniel Ritchie for his helpful comments on the manuscript.

I would also like to acknowledge Ron Beers for his initiation of the Vital Questions series, of which this book is a part, and for his love of books that help people live more faithful lives.

Introduction

Mistrust the man who finds everything good, the man who finds everything evil, and still more the man who is indifferent to everything.

JOHANN K. LAVATER

It is the only serious sin left. Even murder has its mitigating factors, but not this one. It is the pariah sin, the charge that makes you untouchable without need for further explanation. The sin is intolerance and the greatest sinners in twenty-first century America are evangelical and fundamentalist Christians. America is sick of intolerant people and it's not going to tolerate them anymore.

□ □ □ □ □ □ □ □ □ □ □ □ □ □ □ □ □ □ □ □

Tolerance is a much used but little understood term in the ongoing public debate (often referred to in shorthand as the *culture wars*) over what kind of society we are and ought to be. It often arises in conjunction with equally nebulous words such as *diverse, inclusive,* and *multicul-*

tural. It is frequently invoked in the negative—intolerance—and is as strong a word of condemnation as exists in our current public vocabulary. To be branded intolerant confers a kind of social leprosy that makes one unclean in the eyes of some of the most powerful institutions in our land—the schools and universities, the news and entertainment centers, and the courts and halls of government.

Once reserved as a charge against overt racists, religious bigots, and the like, intolerance has undergone a change in definition and application. It has become a useful tool in the culture wars, broadened to apply to almost anyone who has reservations about, much less opposes, the sweeping changes in public and private morality in the last several generations.

> **O**nce reserved as a charge against overt racists, religious bigots, and the like, intolerance has undergone a change in definition and application.

The accusation of intolerance is made most often against moral conservatives—that is, against people who believe that the majority of the notions of right and wrong that have had broad public support (if not always private practice) in the last fifteen hundred years in the Western world are both healthy and reflect something fundamental about the human condition. More specifically, the charge of intolerance is directed at religious people, especially theologically conservative Christians. Those who accuse others of intolerance like to emphasize religion as the source because they are confident that religious values are strictly private and should be kept out of the public sphere. Everyone knows that people don't agree about religion, so it is taken as obvious that religious people ought not to proclaim their values except to each other.

The lines of battle in the culture wars, however, and in issues of tolerance and intolerance, do not divide neatly between conservative and liberal or religious and secular. Moral conservatives may or may not be politically conservative. Many Catholics, for example, are theologically and morally conservative but politically liberal. And moral and political conservatives are not always religious. To add to the confusion, religious people are among those leading the charge for doctrinaire tolerance. Nevertheless, all sides in the culture wars like to simplify things. The main target of the champions of tolerance are Christian conservatives, and the main target of champions of traditional morality are secular liberals. Many others get caught up in the cross fire.

Tolerance Defined

What is there not to like about tolerance? It seems, almost by definition, a good and necessary thing. How can people, whether two or two billion, live together if they cannot tolerate the things in others that they don't like? The need for tolerance grows out of the simple and irreducible fact that there is only one of each of us, and none of us is exactly like another. Because we find some of these differences irritating, we must learn to be tolerant or we will kill each other. That we too often do kill each other as it is points out the importance of basic, unadorned tolerance. We must either get along or be at constant war.

If, by definition, tolerance seems like a good and necessary thing, it is also at the level of definition that the trouble begins. A bare-bones definition of *tolerance* is "putting up with the objectionable."[1] This definition requires us to consider both what we include under *objectionable* and what is entailed in *putting up with*. There

4

is plenty of room in these considerations for raised eyebrows, flared nostrils, and bloodletting—not to mention smug self-righteousness.

The situation is further complicated by the attempts of tolerance advocates to change the definition. We have seen a concerted effort in recent years to change the meaning of *tolerance* from "putting up with the objectionable" to "affirming the diverse." That inversion turns the concept of tolerance on its head and dramatically increases the number of people who can be called intolerant. It is a useful strategy in a culture war, but it does long-range damage to the cause of a healthy and peaceful society.

> **W**e have seen a concerted effort in recent years to change the meaning of *tolerance* from "putting up with the objectionable" to "affirming the diverse."

□ □

How did orthodox Christianity, whose spread throughout the world was based in great part on its inclusiveness ("Come to me, *all* you who are weary"), come to be a symbol of exclusivity and intolerance? The self-congratulating answer echoes the sentiment seen on a church signboard: "If you feel distant from God, guess who moved?" It seems simple—some Christians have stayed true to a 4,000-year-old revelation of moral truth, ultimately rooted in God's eternal character, that offends the "do your own thing" sensibilities of talk-show hosts, Hollywood filmmakers, politically correct editorialists, relativistic intellectuals, and all those who follow their lead.

A less flattering explanation is that the idea of tolerance was the necessary invention of an increasingly secular culture because Christians had the unpleasant habit of slaughtering each other in the name of Christ. Historically, it seems that tolerance was the liberal, practical answer to the inability of conservative religion to compromise even with fellow believers. Unfortunately, that inability to get along has not altogether disappeared. The fiery stakes are gone, but not the fiery rhetoric and spirit of condemnation. Healthy tolerance is as necessary, and in as short supply, in the twenty-first century as it was in the sixteenth.

In many ways the charge of intolerance against Christian conservatives is misguided. It is the inevitable consequence when a people who believe in moral truth try to assert it in a relativistic age that sees all truth as mere opinion. A misguided charge, yes, but not entirely wrong. Christians are often enough belligerent, hostile, and judgmental to have earned the label of intolerant. As with any caricature, there is just enough truth in it to give rise to the caricature in the first place. If our accusers enjoy shooting at us, it is too often we who have provided the ammunition.

In many other ways, however, the question of whether or not we are tolerant misses the point. Tolerance, frankly, is not an explicitly biblical value (though we will see there are many related biblical values). God does not call us to be tolerant, he calls us to love. It is a much higher standard. In the final analysis, we are no more or less intolerant than our critics, but the standards of our critics are too low.

By God's standards, we are worse than intolerant—we often fail

God does not call us to be tolerant, he calls us to love.

to love. And in failing to love, and in failing to shape our actions with love, we fail to be followers of Christ.

Some people think the God of the Bible is intolerant—always condemning, threatening, and punishing. Others think that God may not be intolerant, but his followers certainly are. We will look at both concerns but will begin by seeing where the idea of tolerance has come from, what exactly the term does and does not mean, and how the concept is used in our world today.

A Short History of the Idea of Tolerance

Evil when we are in its power is not felt as evil but as a necessity, or even a duty.

SIMONE WEIL

Intolerance was a problem at least as long ago as Cain and Abel. It has continued ever since, wherever two or three gather together. In biblical history it runs rampant from the Pentateuch to the Prophets—the inability to get along always being part of the story of Israel—and is a recurring headache in the New Testament church. In secular history it is no less the case. Human beings, in small numbers and large, have always had trouble living at peace with each other.

A minimum level of tolerance is necessary for any community to exist, but tolerance did not become an official public policy until the rise of empires. When one small group of people over-

Human beings, in small numbers and large, have always had trouble living at peace with each other.

whelms another, the cultural distinctives of the conquered people are more or less irrelevant. Those distinctives are erased by annihilation or forced assimilation. With the establishment of empires, neither complete annihilation nor assimilation is practical.

Cyrus the Great, for instance, ruled most of what is now called the Middle East in the sixth century B.C. His tolerance of various religions and cultures led him to order the Jews in his kingdom to return to Judah and rebuild Jerusalem and the temple (see Isaiah and Ezra). Later, the Roman Empire, which ruled the entire Mediterranean and beyond, tolerated great diversity in religion and culture as long as the conquered people were compliant and did what they were told. This kind of tolerance was born more of pragmatism than of principle, it being clearly impossible to impose and maintain a uniform culture on a far-flung empire composed of hundreds of different ethnic groups.

Until relatively recent times, the concept of tolerance was applied chiefly to religion and the challenge of dealing with competing religious claims and practices. Christianity, of course, arose during the Roman Empire and was sometimes tolerated and sometimes not. Ironically enough, given the image today of religious people as intolerant, early Christians argued strongly for tolerance at a time when few others did, motivated in part by their own persecution.[1] They were depicted then (as often now) as a threat to society, especially when they refused to offer even token worship of Caesar. Lactantius, an early Christian, was expressing a common Christian view when he argued "there is nothing so voluntary as religion" and pointed out "religion ought to be defended not by killing but by dying." And die for the faith Christians did. They learned to kill for the faith only much later.

Eventually Christianity moved from its status as a tiny, persecuted sect to the official religion of the empire. As that empire waned in the West, Christian institutions, often based on Roman structure, provided an ongoing social glue in a very turbulent era. For a thousand years, church and state together ruled Western society in an often uneasy alliance of ecclesiastical and secular power. Although today we greatly exaggerate the supposedly monocultural quality of medieval Europe, it clearly was not a time of religious pluralism. The Jews were a very small minority (sometimes tolerated, sometimes not), Muslims were perceived only as an *external* threat, usually distant, and other religions were barely known.

In terms of true religious diversity, tolerance wasn't really required in the West for a thousand years. That changed dramatically with the reformation movements of the fifteenth, sixteenth, and seventeenth centuries. The Christian church was split into a bewildering variety of groups, all claiming the anointing of God, and because groups often vied for political power (as the church long had), blood began to flow.

The religious wars in Europe began in the mid-sixteenth century and continued off and on for a hundred years. The underlying forces often were more political than religious, but religion was a convenient way of telling the sides apart, and religious leaders and institutions participated with religious zeal. The numbers of nations participating and noncombatants killed were not surpassed until the world wars of the twentieth century. In the 1572 St. Bartholomew Massacre alone, more than twenty thousand French Protestants were hunted down and slaughtered in only three days. It is not hard to see why, after a hundred years of this, reasonable and even godly people wanted a new way of settling religious and political differences.

The word used during this time was *toleration,* rather than tolerance, and the focus was almost entirely on religion. *Toleration* was the belief that governments should not attempt to settle religious disputes or force a common religious belief and practice on an entire society. The consensus before this time was that social order depended on shared values and views, which to a certain extent seems like common sense. Unity in a society was thought to require unity in, among other things, religious belief. Religious dissent was not only a theological or ecclesiastical problem, it was also seen as a threat to the stability of the state.

A century of bloodshed, however, convinced people that enforcing religious unanimity was itself contributing to instability and disorder. People were exhausted, disgusted, and ready for a new paradigm (which in fact was a very old paradigm rediscovered). Religion increasingly was seen as a private matter to be settled by the exercise of private conscience, and toleration became in time the common wisdom.

While the influence of religious faith on society and even government remained strong, the rise of toleration in the sixteenth and seventeenth centuries played an important part in the growing secularization of society that has continued to the present day. The practical move of allowing, for the sake of public peace, a degree of religious pluralism in the seventeenth century was augmented in the eigh-

A century of bloodshed, however, convinced people that enforcing religious unanimity was itself contributing to instability and disorder.

teenth century by the continuing rise of science and rationalism to form a challenge to traditional faith. An informed agnosticism or atheism became a viable public alternative in the nineteenth century, and by the end of the twentieth century, religion was considered by many shapers of culture to be either repugnant or irrelevant.

It is no wonder then that current attempts by people of faith to introduce their values into the public debate are often met with astonishment and anger. Many powerful people today see the secularization of society and the suppression of the influence of religion as a crucial sign of human progress. They offer a crude and simplistic, but not altogether fabricated, version of religious history that emphasizes oppression, bloodshed, and, yes, intolerance. They see themselves as representatives of reason, goodwill, and the fight against injustice—and traditional religion as a primitive force always ready to drag civilization back to darker times.

Religion, in this common view, should only speak publicly when it speaks the language and affirms the values of the secular, progressive culture. Traditional religious belief, especially when it can be attached to a label such as the Religious Right, is seen not only as offending reason and secular mores but also as violating a centuries-old agreement, said to be reinforced in our own Constitution, to keep religion in the private sphere. Perceived religious intolerance, then, is an offense against both decades of effort to erase social injustice (which the church is accused of having supported) and against the very idea of a free democratic society in which no one imposes his or her views on another.

Such sweeping summaries of cultural history are of limited value. But even this brief overview helps explain some of the heat that is generated when issues of tolerance arise, especially when so

many of those issues seem to deal with private behavior. Those who see the flow of history as mov-
ing toward greater and greater individual
freedom resent attempts to enforce a common
and, in their minds, badly outdated morality.

Moral conservatives, of course, see it differently.
Many of them argue that the Judeo-Christian emphasis on the individual value of every person as a
creation of God has been the motivating—if inconsistent—force for much of the progress in human
freedom over the centuries. They see rising secular-
ism as undercutting the very intellectual and spiritual foundations on which concepts such as justice
and goodness are based.
They are shocked by
how quickly a public
consensus on basic
moral issues has col-
lapsed and decry the
tremendous social cost
of moral confusion. At
the very least, they do
not understand why
they are called ugly
names when, like everyone else, they stand up for
their values in public.

> **M**oral conservatives argue
> that the Judeo-Christian
> emphasis on the individual
> value of every person as a
> creation of God has been
> the motivating—if inconsis-
> tent—force for much of the
> progress in human freedom
> over the centuries.

2 What *Is* Tolerance?
Definitions and Distinctions

*Tolerance is only complacence when it makes no
distinction between right and wrong.*

SARAH PATTON BOYLE

Make no mistake, the basic conflict over issues of
tolerance and intolerance does not exist because
people don't understand each other. Most often
there is a direct clash of profoundly different values and ways of seeing and assessing the world.
Nevertheless, much of the heated rhetoric arises
because of a failure to understand terms and
make necessary distinctions. Some of this is in-
tentional, there being advantages in a dispute to
keeping terms fuzzy, but more of it is a simple
failure to think clearly and historically. Like
many slogan words, the term *tolerance* has been
manipulated and abused.

As we have seen, *tolerance,* or *toleration,* was
originally used only in the context of religious diversity. It grew in meaning to apply to all areas of
disagreement and, in time, became a very general

and positive term that suggested a certain approach to life. The essential meaning of the word, however, did not change; it was simply more widely applied. In our own time, however, an attempt has been made, largely successfully, to empty the word of its traditional meaning and replace it with a meaning that is almost its opposite. In light of that, we do well to look at definitions and distinctions.

To understand tolerance, one must understand that tolerance requires objection. The word derives from a Latin word, *tolerare,* meaning "to bear or endure." A handy working definition of *tolerance* is "putting up with the objectionable." At the very heart of tolerance, ironically, is a moment of intolerance— of refusing to agree. What makes tolerance tolerant is that it does not fully act on this

A handy working definition of *tolerance* is "putting up with the objectionable."

objection. That is, it decides, in varying degrees, to coexist with this thing to which it objects, rather than try to eliminate it.

If you do not object to something, you cannot be said to be tolerant of it. This is important in our public discussions of tolerance because so many people mistakenly claim to be tolerant in areas where they have no objection. Most social liberals, for instance, cannot rightfully be said to be tolerant regarding ho-mosexual behavior since they have no ob-

If you do not object to something, you cannot be said to be tolerant of it.

jection to it. You do not have to tolerate that which you accept or affirm.

Furthermore, if tolerance requires an initial objection, it also implies withheld power. If I *would* eliminate something if I could but am powerless to do so, I am not tolerant, merely impotent. True tolerance means I *voluntarily* withhold what power I have to coerce someone else's behavior or suppress an idea. This has special relevance in an open society such as ours, where a wide range of divergent thinking and behavior is protected by law and custom. In such a society, one must show varying degrees of tolerance even to that to which one objects.

If tolerance is not the same as acceptance, it is also not the same as indifference. If I don't care about something one way or another, I am not tolerant of it because, again, I do not object to it. A challenge for those who prize tolerance as one of the highest public goods, in fact, is to distinguish between healthy tolerance and a diseased moral passivity or indifference. What is the difference between a genuinely tolerant society and a morally bankrupt one, incapable of and uninterested in calling evil what it is?

There actually is a wide range of responses to behaviors and ideas that are often confused with tolerance but in fact are something else. Think of these responses on a continuum similar to a number line with negative and positive numbers. At the positive extreme of the continuum is celebration of the behavior or idea. At the negative extreme is action to eliminate the idea or behavior. At the zero or midpoint of this continuum lies tolerance. To its left is indifference and then rejection heading toward elimination. To its right is acceptance and then affirmation heading toward celebration.[1]

Genuine *in*tolerance begins with rejection. It entails a refusal to put up with, or tolerate, that thing to which it objects. It works actively to eliminate that thing to the extent that it has the power to do so. But it would tend to make this effort within the normal boundaries of law and by socially acceptable means. (Someone who is intolerant of racism, for instance, would work to eliminate it but would not try to assassinate the head of the Ku Klux Klan.)

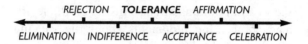

On the other side of tolerance is acceptance. It has a mildly positive attitude toward the behavior or idea in question and is thereby distinguished from true tolerance. Beyond it is affirmation, a clear preference for something that tends to result in action to promote it, just as rejection results in action to eliminate something. That same person who rejects racism may not only be accepting of ethnic minorities, he or she may work actively to promote their welfare.

At the extremes lie celebration and elimination. Either of these can motivate actions that go beyond law and normal bounds of human effort. Both are far removed from the nuanced, mixed impulses of tolerance with its tension between rejection and acceptance.

Some have suggested other continuums that help one better understand tolerance. One scholar identifies tolerance as the midpoint between absolutism and an insistence on uniformity at one end and relativism and the rejection of value judgments at the other.[2] Tolerance recognizes the fact and the value of having a variety of views and opinions but also insists on the legitimacy of making judgments about the varying worth or truthfulness of each one.

Seeing tolerance as a middle position between extremes does not automatically make it preferable to any other position, including an extreme position. One cannot make the judgment that tolerance is a good thing until one knows what one is being asked to tolerate. This is a crucial point that will be more fully explored later.

If tolerance is not automatically a good thing (Germans were wrong to tolerate Nazism in the early 1930s, for example), then intolerance is not automatically a bad thing. Just as we must make distinctions between tolerance and other concepts it is confused with, so we must reject an automatic equation of intolerance with, for instance, prejudice and bigotry.

> **O**ne cannot make the judgment that tolerance is a good thing until one knows what one is being asked to tolerate.

Prejudice is judging without adequate data or

reflection. It means *pre*-judgment, making a judgment about something or someone before one has earned the right to do so, that is, before one knows enough. Because it involves prejudgment, prejudice is automatically wrong *even if* the judgment is correct. *Bigotry,* while it involves intolerance, also adds a psychological dimension of obstinance, unreflectiveness, and even hate.

Intolerance, on the other hand, may well be the position one comes to after long and careful thought. I can weigh issues, use reason, apply moral principles, even show compassion, and then decide not to tolerate something (like human cloning, for instance). I may end up being intolerant, but I have not been prejudiced or bigoted.

The error of prejudice—prejudgment—should not frighten us away from making appropriate judgments. Judgment is a good and needed thing and is a synonym for discernment. We should not confuse it with the related word *judgmental.* *Judgmental,* like *bigoted,* is a word that suggests a distortion of true judgment by a spirit of condemnation. (The same is true for the word *discrimination,* a positive term for making careful and reasonable distinctions between things, which now has only negative connotations for many people.)

Carefully evaluating something and either approving or disapproving of it is an example of necessary judgment, discernment, and discrimination. We need more of it, not less.

The point here is not that intolerance is a good thing or that it is never associated with prejudice, bigotry, and hate. It often is. The point is that one cannot evaluate either tolerance or intolerance without looking at real-life situations. *What* is being tolerated or not tolerated and in what spirit and with what consequences?

We do ourselves harm when we pretend that different things are actually the same. Physical life is not possible without distinctions (a very slight change in the carbon atom and life would not be possible), and the same is true of our moral, spiritual, and intellectual lives. If we allow distinctions to be blurred or erased when it comes to tolerance, we injure ourselves and our communities.

Degrees of Tolerance and Intolerance

Just as one should distinguish between tolerance and related but different terms, so one can and should make many other distinctions in this debate. One can distinguish, as conservative Christians like to do, between a person and a behavior. It is possible, though often difficult, to love a person and hate what that person does, as when a parent loves a son but hates his drug use and thievery. Notice that in this case both ends of the continuum between celebration and elimination are in play at the same time.

Yet even within the single category of tolerance there is a range of possible responses that vary according to the precise nature of one's objection and the degree to which one acts on it. Even if I tolerate something, I must decide what form my tolerance will take. Should I mentally disapprove but not act? act by advocating against the thing to which I object but not try to censor or legally sup-

> **Yet even within the single category of tolerance there is a range of possible responses that vary according to the precise nature of one's objection and the degree to which one acts on it.**

press it? act through persuasion to effect voluntary change or change of heart?

For instance, one could believe that homosexual behavior is a sign of brokenness or sin and oppose the attempt to normalize it yet still believe homosexuals have all the worth and rights of other human beings. This would be an example of tolerance—objecting yet putting up with.

Another might agree but refuse the right to marriage. A third might agree to *most* rights but believe homosexuals should not be hired as teachers. Yet another would add that a landlord has a right to deny homosexuals housing.

Each of these positions is an example of tolerance, but the first is objection leaning toward acceptance and the last is objection leaning toward rejection. In our public exchanges, however, *all* of the above positions on homosexual practice would be branded as intolerant by current champions of tolerance. There is little if any recognition of significant distinctions in the culture wars because distinctions are not seen as helping win battles.

And perhaps Christian fundamentalists would feel the same if one of them were the tolerated party. There is a range of tolerance, for instance, among secularists regarding religious faith. Some think religious belief mistaken but respect religious people. Others think religion is acceptable in the world but would not want an overtly religious person as a coworker. Still others work toward eliminating the influence of religion but would not outlaw it. All of these are tolerant of religion to a varying degree, but it might not all feel like tolerance to someone who takes faith seriously.

Why Tolerate Wrong?

No one, when pressed, believes tolerance to be an absolute good. All agree that some things should not be tolerated. This raises the question, "Why, in fact, should one want to be tolerant at all?" If one objects to something, especially if one believes it is evil or harmful or in error— or all three together— then why not seek to eliminate it by all means possible? Why should one tolerate that which one believes is morally evil (like pornography or social injustice) or leads to evil (like drug use)?

No one, when pressed, believes tolerance to be an absolute good.

Isn't *tolerating* evil just a soft name for *doing* evil? (Secularists like the Marxist philosopher Herbert Marcuse have taken this position, as do many religious fundamentalists.)

For most of human history, as we have seen, this is exactly what the majority believed. The more uniform a culture is—in race, language, religion, political thought, custom, and all the other things that define a culture—the easier it is to reject all that deviates from the norm. Intolerance—in ancient China or Greece or in medieval Europe—did not receive the condemnation that it does today because it seemed both normal and logical to defend what was agreed to be right and good.

"Agreed" is the problematic word. Where a cultural consensus is challenged, as it increasingly was in Renaissance and Reformation Europe for instance, one must either resort to ever greater force to suppress dissent, or one must agree to disagree.

As the need for tolerance was ever more strongly felt, the rationales for tolerance were developed to answer our question, "Why tolerate wrong?" One of the strongest, especially in the religious realm, is the self-evident truth that co-

erced belief is not belief at all, something persecuted Christians had argued during the first days
of Christianity. God is not honored and does not
even accept faith that comes at the point of a
sword. So why force Jews to convert or Anabap-
tists to accept infant baptism?

This raises another important distinction. In
calls for tolerance, one can focus on external behavior or on internal states of mind. The Romans
didn't particularly care what early Christians believed about God as long as they were willing to
ceremonially recognize the divinity of Caesar.
They were tolerant of deviant internal beliefs but
intolerant of deviant external behaviors. Modern
promoters of tolerance have set themselves a
much higher—some argue impossible—standard. They not only work to eliminate intolerance in laws and common practices, they seek to
identify and eliminate it in thoughts, attitudes,
and subtle gestures. They have a Puritan-like
concern for monitoring and cleansing inner states
of being, and a Puritan-like pessimism that the
cleansing is ever wholly successful.

Another classic defense of tolerance, found in
writers like John Locke in the seventeenth century and John Stuart Mill in the nineteenth cen-

tury, flows out of an emphasis on the autonomy of the individual. A general trend in Western intellectual and social history for the last five hundred years has been a growing emphasis on the primacy of private, individual judgment and a parallel decline in the authority of persons and institutions that lie outside the individual.

We have increasingly insisted on the right to decide for ourselves all questions large and small rather than automatically accept the more community-wide decisions of tradition or institutions. In short, we have increasingly insisted that our personal view, whether mainstream or idiosyncratic, should be both socially tolerated and legally protected.

This insistence on the right to one's own views and values carries with it, of course, the requirement to respect the similar rights of others. The result should be a general environment of tolerance, thought to be advantageous for individuals and communities alike.

> In short, we have increasingly insisted that our personal view, whether mainstream or idiosyncratic, should be both socially tolerated and legally protected.

Closely related to this emphasis on individual judgment is the defense of tolerance based on humility. Mill argues that we can never be sure that the view that we reject is in fact false or that our own is true. Therefore we should not try to suppress an idea that differs from our own because there may be as much or more truth in that idea as in ours. We can argue against it, but we should let it be heard.

Even if we are quite sure of the rightness of our position, there are reasons to tolerate some kinds of evil and error. The refusal to tolerate an evil, for example, sometimes creates an even greater evil. Fighting heresy by burning people at the stake took people's lives unfairly and did nothing helpful to further the cause of orthodoxy. It was both wrong and useless.

Similarly, setting up strong censorship laws to suppress genuinely dangerous ideas can also result in the suppression of greatly valuable ideas. For the sake of the valuable ideas we tolerate the dangerous or deluded ones. This doesn't mean we can't oppose error, only that we must oppose it in a way that does not fall into even greater error.

Mill had great confidence, perhaps a naive confidence, that truth will always win out in the long run in a contest with error. He believed human reason would, over time, sort out the good from the bad and follow the good. This view was easier to hold amidst the optimism of the nineteenth century than it is after the genocide, totalitarianism, materialism, and terrorism of the twentieth and twenty-first centuries. A religious conservative might argue that Mill was right to emphasize humility, but that he should have applied that recognition of human limitations both to human reason and to the ability of the human will to follow the good even when it is apparent.

□ □

This raises some of the long-standing arguments *against* uncritical tolerance. One is rooted in the distinction between ideas and behaviors. Ideas cannot be separated from actions. Ideas, attitudes, and beliefs are inextricably linked to behaviors. There is no important idea that does not in some way shape behavior. The effect of those behaviors in turn cannot be limited to the individual. Individual choices have community consequences.

Immoral and dangerous ideas, according to this argument, encourage immoral and dangerous behavior, very little of which can be antiseptically walled off so that it affects only the individuals who participate in those behaviors. Think of the society-wide effects of drug abuse, sexual license, child pornography, racism, and the like. It is naive and irresponsible to argue

Individual choices have community consequences.

that something should be tolerated simply because an individual's ideas and behaviors are no one else's business.

It is the corporate effects of individual ideas and actions that make it so difficult to decide when and how much to tolerate. Unfortunately, wrong is often persuasive. One may think, *I do not have to worry about this idea or behavior because I can simply refuse it*. But many times the concern is not that this will directly damage me, but that, being persuasive, it will influence and harm others, including children. Do I defend the right of neo-Nazis, for instance, to hold rallies and distribute literature, based on the recognition that I need the same right to express my own views? Or do I say, "Since history has shown these ideas to be powerful and deadly, they must not even be allowed to be expressed"?

□ □ □ □ □ □ □ □ □ □ □ □ □ □ □ □ □ □ □

Even with the rise of tolerance in the last three hundred years, and its virtual deification in the last thirty, it has always been widely acknowledged, as we have seen, that no moral person tolerates everything. For some, the intolerable grows largely from issues relating to justice and fairness—racism, sexism, abortion, homophobia, economic inequity. Such people are sometimes divided on an issue like pornography, in which equally held values—freedom of expression and opposition to the exploitation of women—collide.

For others, the list of things that should at least be objected to, and perhaps not tolerated, is much longer. One could argue that given the definition of tolerance as putting up with the objectionable, social conservatives are in fact much more tolerant than social liberals because there are so many more things to which they object. The *least* tolerant person is the one who accepts everything, because such a person is not required to overcome any internal objections. (Regarding the call to be broad-minded—the tolerance slogan of his day— G. K. Chesterton observed that turnips are singularly broad-minded.)

Since everyone agrees that some things should not be tolerated, the real issue is not whether you are tolerant or intolerant, but what's included on your list. Certain things, we all agree, should be tolerated and other things should not. But we don't agree on what goes on which list, or on what we should do about those things on which we differ.

Both tolerance and intolerance can be healthy if they are based on sound principle, not on either indifference or prejudice. If my objection to something grows out of prejudice, bigotry, ignorance, or mean-spiritedness, it is wrong, even if the thing I object to is also wrong. Likewise, if I tolerate something because of indifference, passivity, or moral paralysis, that seeming tolerance (for it isn't actually tolerance at all) is wrong, even if the thing I tolerate *should* be tolerated.

J. Budziszewski offers a helpful summation: healthy tolerance entails "the wisdom to know which bad things to put up with, when, why, and to what degree—along with the strength of character to act on that wisdom."[3] We can make the mistake of not putting up with enough, he points out, and we can also make the mistake of putting up with too much. It takes discernment to know the difference and moral courage to act on that discernment.

The Appeal of Tolerance for Contemporary Values

Tolerance is one of the few universally commended virtues in our society. That it is considered a virtue, rather than a pragmatic attitude, is itself revealing. It has gained its status both because it seems a basic requirement for a free and open society and because it appeals to a core of related contemporary values.

One of those values, as we have seen, is the autonomy of the individual. My individual judgments and behaviors should not be suppressed in the name of something higher, because there *is* nothing higher. Or if there is, it is my job to factor in that higher something, not yours. To do so is intolerant.

Similarly, as an autonomous individual, my primary responsibility is to maximize my potential (without, of course, harming others). Therefore it is necessary that I be able to explore various possibilities for myself, including those you might consider deviant or harmful. Because I am autonomous, neither you nor society is in a position to rightfully deny me my quest for self-actualization. To do so is intolerant.

Furthermore, this individual self-fulfillment is in keeping with a third central contemporary value—diversity. In a world where there are countless different cultures, all expressing different values and attitudes and behaviors, it is not only necessary that we be tolerant, but it is morally incumbent upon us to celebrate all those differences and all that diversity. To do any less is to be intolerant.

Each of these values—individualism, self-actualization, and diversity—is affirmed by both conservatives and liberals, by both the religious and the secular. Each, however, is an abstraction, and each is understood and applied differently in specific situations. Just as I cannot tell you if I am tolerant until you tell me specifically what I am asked to tolerate, so I cannot give a blank approval of diversity, for instance, until you tell me what example of diversity is being contemplated.

Context is everything when it comes to questions of tolerance and intolerance. And the single most important thing to understand about the context in which the current tolerance debate takes place is the concept of relativism. We live in a relativistic age; it is the air we breathe. It shapes both the pronouncement and reception of all public claims of what is good and true.

Relativism is the view that all truth claims are rooted in opinion, not in fact or in the nature of things. If I say, "This is true" or "This is wrong" (with some exceptions allowed for the natural sciences and mathematics), I am stating a personal opinion. My opinion has been formed by my society and my personal experience. It is a blend of inherited beliefs and personal experiences, feelings, and reasonings. The result has authority for me, for the moment at least, but no necessary authority for anyone else.

Context is everything when it comes to questions of tolerance and intolerance.

As elsewhere, it is important to make distinctions. Relativism is related to but not the same as pluralism. Pluralism is based on the clearly observable fact that there are many different views and values and practices in the world. It tends to believe that the existence of this diversity is a good thing or at least acceptable, but pluralism is an observation, not an evaluation. It makes no evaluation of diverse views and values, but neither does it prohibit such evaluations.

Relativism, on the other hand, does exactly that. Relativism absolutizes pluralism. It takes the fact of the diversity of outlooks—pluralism—and draws the illegitimate and illogical conclusion that because there are many views no one of them is any better than any other. From the clear fact that we cannot agree on what is true, it wrongly deduces that there is therefore no truth—only opinions. The spirit of relativism is expressed succinctly in a dictum offered approvingly in my son's high school sociology text as it discussed homosexual practice: "Everything is right somewhere and nothing is right everywhere."

It is easy to see how this view leads to tolerance becoming one of the highest social goods. It is Mill's humility taken to the ultimate extreme. All notions of what is true and good are the product of individuals and individual cultures. There is no standard above culture—rational, religious, or natural—by which to judge between one view and another. Therefore the highest priority must be placed on not advancing any one view or value over another.

Relativism has been shown by many philosophers, including those who are no friends of religion, to be self-contradictory and logically insipid. For starters, relativism exempts itself from its own view, making relativism an absolute truth in a world where supposedly there are none. If there is no truth, relativism is not true.

Demonstrating the bankruptcy of an idea, however, only rarely diminishes its use. The *spirit* of relativism, especially when not overtly named, is very powerful in our time precisely because it is so useful. And one of its uses, as we will see, is to bloody those who espouse traditional morality.

It is important to distinguish between relativism in the abstract and garden-variety relativism as it expresses itself in everyday life. Technically a pure relativist would not believe in tolerance, because a pure and consistent relativist would never object to anything. But no one is a pure relativist. It is an approach to life barely compatible with survival.

Those most likely to accuse others of intolerance are generally not consistent relativists. They advocate many values—as they should—and they are confident that the positions they advocate are superior to those they oppose. Like many people in our time, however, they are often *functional* relativists. While making many value and truth claims themselves, they retreat to a kind of knee-jerk relativism when pressed by a moral claim that makes them uncomfortable. Perhaps the most common expression of this retreat is the ubiquitous question, "Who are you to say?"

And even if few are willing to call themselves relativists, many act and believe as does the intellectual who confidently observes that the relativity of values is now "a matter of urbanity and manners, and only a bigot or pedant can ignore it."[4] It simply isn't civilized not to be, shall we say, flexible about these things.

The inconsistent but pervasive relativism of our time is the unacknowledged basis for many of the charges of intolerance against moral conservatives, but it actually is itself the enemy of a healthy tolerance. It erodes the grounds for objecting to *anything*—including racism, sexism, homophobia, and the like—and contributes to the loss of the ability to distinguish between good and evil that any society needs to survive.

The noted essayist Lance Morrow reflects on

our weakened ability to speak up against the disgusting:

> What once would have been intolerable and impermissible in public conduct now has become commonplace. If it is not exactly accepted, then at least it is abjectly and wearily endured. Social habit in the United States has taken decisive turns toward the awful. . . . Somehow, Americans also have displaced the moral confidence with which to condemn sleaziness and stupidity. It is as if something in the American judgment snapped, and has remained so long unrepaired that no one notices anymore.[5]

Our judgment did not so much "snap" as it rotted, slowly but inexorably corroding in the acid of relativism. When we no longer allowed ourselves to say "This is true," we robbed ourselves of the moral confidence to say "This is wrong."

A Healthy Notion of Tolerance

Tolerance, then, is neither a good nor a bad thing in itself. Its moral status varies depending on what is being tolerated. There is, however, a healthy understanding of tolerance that is both a good in itself and an absolute necessity for any society. It is a conception that has developed over a long history of human conflict and is a kind of minimum response to our tendency toward fear, anger, insecurity, and violence. It presents a largely secular face in contemporary culture but rightfully receives the blessing of religion, out of which it ultimately springs.

This understanding of tolerance is difficult to describe in a few words but goes something like this. Each person is valuable. The person who believes we are all made and valued by God has a more logical basis for asserting this than does someone who believes we are derived solely from chemical processes, but everyone agrees that humans have value. Because we are valuable, it matters what happens to us.

Each person is also unique—and so are families, neighborhoods, nations, and cultures. Uniqueness is rightly celebrated (being a product of God's creativity), but in a fallen world it carries with it the potential for conflict.

Without belaboring the obvious, it is clear that I, as a unique being, will often encounter ideas and behaviors to which I object—in my wife, my children, my colleagues, and in the world at large. Sometimes my objections will be rational and sometimes nonrational or even irrational. Sometimes people will simply "bug me" and I won't be able to explain my "objection" beyond that. On other occasions, my objection will be principled and profound.

A healthy notion of tolerance requires us to put up with the vast majority of these objections. We accept, as we should, that others think and act differently than we do, and although we may not like or affirm it, we do tolerate it. If we didn't, life would be an endless series of irresolvable conflicts, small and large. (And for severely intolerant people, it is so.)

This minimum kind of tolerance, then, is rooted as much in pragmatism as in principle. It operates by a kind of greatly watered-down Golden Rule: tolerate others so that they will tolerate you. It is expressed in Rodney King's poignant question in the midst of riots: "Can't we get along?" Without this kind of tolerance, brothers and sisters quarrel, marriages fall apart, friendships split, and societies dissolve in figurative or literal civil war.

This is tolerance at its most basic. Everyone practices it to one degree or another, and everyone can agree that we need more of it. People of character and faith, as we will see, are called to a much higher standard than this. We cannot reach that higher standard, however, if we are not capable of meeting this lower one.

This minimum kind of tolerance operates by a kind of greatly watered-down Golden Rule: tolerate others so that they will tolerate you.

And even though I have argued that intolerance is not automatically a good or bad thing, there is nonetheless a kind of intolerance that is ugly and diseased and all too common. This intolerance is not based on rationally and morally defendable principles but is characterized by attributes like suspicion, mean-spiritedness, aggressive ignorance, close-mindedness, primitive anger, refusal to dialogue, and the like. It commonly manifests itself in things like racism, mindless nationalism, religious and antireligious bigotry, and finds its logical conclusion in hate. It is condemned by any morally serious person.

This kind of intolerance is not only psychologically deforming, it also prevents one from seeing things truthfully. Reinhold Niebuhr has this form in mind when he describes religious fanaticism as "religious loyalties so restrictive as to present false visions of reality which make it impossible for the 'religious' person to live in mutuality and respect with any person not sharing his religious commitments."[6] And, of course, the description fits any fanaticism, religious or secular.

□ □ □ □ □ □ □ □ □ □ □ □ □ □ □ □ □ □ □

If by tolerant, someone means a healthy notion of tolerance as a willingness to get along, then I want to be tolerant. In fact, I want to be more than merely tolerant. I want to affirm most of the diversity in the world, especially since I believe most of it was created by God.

If by tolerant, however, one means unable or unwilling to make moral judgments or to believe in truth, then I must decline to be tolerant. This diseased understanding of tolerance is as dangerous as a diseased kind of intolerance, perhaps more so.

3 The Use and Misuse of Tolerance in the Culture Wars

The devil hath power to assume a pleasing shape.
WILLIAM SHAKESPEARE, *HAMLET*

It is not enough to understand dictionary definitions of terms and the distinctions between them. There is often a great difference between what terms mean in the dictionary (and in history) and how they are actually used in everyday life. There are two main reasons why the issue of tolerance is so often heated and confused today. The first is that people always have and always will disagree on what should be tolerated and what should not. The second is that a concerted effort has been made to change basic definitions.

In all debates, the person who controls the definitions controls the debate. If I get to define what tolerance and intolerance are, it is quite easy to ensure that I end up on the side of the good guys and all my enemies on the side of the bad guys.

It is crucial for the health of any society, however, that definitions of important concepts are not manipulated for the sake of short-term ideological gain. If we allow words to mean whatever anyone wants them to mean at a given moment, we soon lose the ability to talk to each other and not being able to talk is much worse than disagreeing.

There is plenty of blame to go around in the culture wars, but the blame for trying to change the definitions of key terms lies mainly with those who champion tolerance as a great personal virtue and social good. Essentially they have turned the concept on its head by defining tolerance not as putting up with the objectionable but as affirming the diverse. By doing so, they have emptied the term of its historical meaning and rendered it useless as a term of either praise or blame.

One example among legions of this change of definition can be seen in the seemingly innocuous decision of the United Nations to declare 1995 "The Year of Tolerance."[1] Who would protest? But look at their definition of tolerance: "respect, acceptance and appreciation of the rich diversity of our world's cultures, our forms of expression and ways of being human." This is a wonderful thing, but it has nothing to do with the traditional meaning of tolerance. There is no objection here—and therefore no tolerance. This is celebration. The UN was right to affirm these things, but they should have called it "The Year of Affirmation."

Changing the definition of tolerance goes hand in hand with a series of related strategies. One strategy is to make the concept entirely and automatically positive, rather than morally neutral as it actually is. If tolerance is, by definition, good, then one who is labeled intolerant can be seen to be, by definition, bad. Intolerance can then be used interchangeably with terms like hate, bigotry, and prejudice.

The tactic is especially effective if repugnance to the concept is so reflexive that one does not even have to think in order to know how one should respond. Calling someone intolerant can have the same instant effect that one might achieve in other times and places

If tolerance is, by definition, good, then one who is labeled intolerant can be seen to be, by definition, bad.

49

by calling someone a leper, communist, capitalist, or heretic—or that the labels homosexual or fundamentalist elicit in different circles today.

We discussed earlier an unhealthy form of intolerance characterized by mean-spiritedness, ignorance, anger, and the like. It is this kind of intolerance that the champions of tolerance want you to have in mind whenever they call someone intolerant. They do not want you to ask yourself, "Is the intolerance in this case justifiable, principled, even potentially good?" They want you to hear the word *intolerant,* know that it is bad, and react accordingly.

And, of course, defenders of traditional values often do similar things. In a war, you want soldiers to react to commands, not do a lot of original thinking.

Another strategy when trying to persuade the general public is the use of slogans. Slogans have at least two advantages: they reduce something complex to something simple, and they are easy to remember. Some common slogans in the tolerance wars are worth evaluating.

The most common slogan, mentioned earlier, comes in the form of a question: "Who are you to say?" This question, the first thing that comes to the mind and lips of the average person when confronted with a moral assertion they find distasteful, is an example of the unconscious, reflexive relativism that is so widespread in the modern world. It seems to be a question rooted in healthy tolerance, but it actually signals a retreat from necessary moral judgment.

The most common slogan ...: "Who are you to say?"

The unstated assumption behind the question is that it is impossible to agree on a common moral standard from which to judge. Therefore it is illogical as well as unethical to make moral assertions about other people's behavior.

Though it is presented as an unanswerable question meant to shame people out of their seeming judgmentalism, the question actually is easily and appropriately answered. Perhaps the most fundamental answer is "I am a human being." Being a human being, living among other human beings, gives one both rights and responsibilities. One of the responsibilities is to engage in the public dialogue about what makes for a good society.

Those who try to short-circuit that dialogue by asking "Who are you to say?" are the ones who should have to explain themselves.

Any person has the right to answer "I am a human being," but a Jew or Christian could also add "I am a human being made in the image of God." Inherent in being made in the image of God is having moral capacities and moral responsibilities. We have the ability, admittedly fallible, to make judgments about right and wrong, and we have the responsibility to do so. It is one thing, among others, that distinguishes us from animals. Asserting that capacity and responsibility does not prove one's position is right, but it does reveal the absurdity of someone implying that these things are beyond moral analysis.

One can also answer the "Who are you to say?" question with another question: "I am the same person who speaks against racism, sexism, and the abuse of children—do you think I have a right to speak against these things?" This response exposes the basic hypocrisy of the slogan. Those who use it make endless assertions themselves about how people should and should not behave. They are right to do so, but they are hypocrites to suggest that you should not.

Finally, this slogan is not only hypocritical, it is also naive. No society could exist if it did not make endless public moral judgments—about everything from traffic laws (speeding is a moral issue because it endangers others) to social policy. And if such a society could exist, you wouldn't want to live in it. We all have "to say" and, in one way or another, most of us do.

A second popular slogan that springs readily to the lips takes the form of a complaint rather than a question. Intolerant people are said to be "trying to force their values" on the rest of us. Again, there is an unstated appeal to relativism here. Values are thought to be radically individual, unverifiable, and in conflict. To argue for any one value or set of values is an offense against individualism, freedom, and the American way.

Intolerant people are said to be "trying to force their values" on the rest of us.

And again, the hypocrisy is not difficult to see. The same people who lament others "forcing their values" are usually eager for their own values to prevail. To the extent that their own values have already prevailed (with current abortion law, for example), it is convenient to pretend that the status quo is in fact a neutral position and that any attempt to change it is a case of someone "forcing their values." At one time legalized slavery was the status quo. Were those who sought to overthrow it "forcing their values" on society? Of course. Should they have said, "We personally do not approve of owning slaves, but we will not force our values on those who do"?

As with the "Who are you to say?" slogan, the "forcing values" argument is also naive as well as hypocritical. Modern cultures are boiling cauldrons of divergent ideas, worldviews, social agendas, political visions, values, and marketing strategies. There is endless competition for the hearts and minds (and wallets) of every sentient being. It is called the marketplace, and we all are part of it.

At one time moral conservatives had a much bigger voice in the marketplace. Their voice now is quite small, but it cannot and should not be silenced, least of all by vacuous "Who are you to say?" or "forcing your values" slogans. What group is *not* trying to have its values and vision become normative? Do feminists shy away from "forcing their values"? Republicans or Democrats? Greenpeace? Filmmakers and novelists? Intellectuals and academics? Advertising agencies? The same people who rightly value diversity and listening to many voices, frequently want to lessen diversity when they don't like what some of those voices are saying.

Those who use these slogans in the name of tolerance are actually practicing their own form of intolerance. They do not really trust diversity and the free exchange of ideas to ensure that their own values will win out. Therefore they find it necessary not simply to argue against the ideas of moral conservatives, which is perfectly legitimate, but to try to keep those ideas from even being seriously considered by ruling them out-of-bounds by definition. Contesting ideas and values gives way to the suppression of ideas and values, and of course moral conservatives sometimes do the same thing.

Those who use these slogans in the name of tolerance are actually practicing their own form of intolerance.

□ □ □ □ □ □ □ □ □ □ □ □ □ □ □ □ □ □ □

There are certain areas where Christian conservatives attract the most fire for supposedly forcing their values on others. The two most prominent are the broad area of sexual conduct (ranging from abortion to pornography to homosexual practice) and the insistence on proselytizing. I will briefly consider only the second because it highlights how far the gospel of tolerance has gone in distorting the cultural dialogue.

America seems unable to get over the fact that Baptists want to save people. I scan the news headlines and discover the shocking story that a Baptist national convention has reaffirmed its belief in hell—and therefore in the need for saving the lost. A guest commentator on National Public Radio surprised even his progressive hosts, but spoke for many, when he reacted to this Southern Baptist effrontery: "The evaporation of four million [people] who believe in this crap would leave the world a better place."[2] So much for tolerance and diversity.

Another recent headline announces that Baptists are making a special effort to pray for Hindus, and the story quotes concerned mainline clergy saying that this is the kind of intolerance that gives Christianity a bad name. References to the Spanish Inquisition are usually not far behind.

The assumptions, sometimes stated but usually not, are the familiar ones. All religions are equally valid. Trying to persuade someone to change his or her religious convictions is a form of cultural imperialism and, in addition, shows a lack of respect for that person. Only narrow, close-minded, ignorant people try to do such intolerant things.

The possible responses are many. First, one can use the same diversity argument often used against religious conservatives. We should allow Baptists to be Baptists the same way we allow elephants to be large. Evangelizing is at the core of what Baptists, and many other Christians, believe and are commanded to do. Baptists not only try to convert Hindus, they try to convert each other. Asking a Baptist not to evangelize is like asking an Orthodox Jew not to believe there is only one God, or a socialist not to believe in the distribution of wealth, or a feminist not to believe in a woman's right to vote.

Second, if we really believe in an open society,

we have to allow others the right to try to change us. We, in turn, have the right to hang up on them, boycott their meetings, not read their material, slam the door in their faces, not donate to their fund-raisers, tell them they are jerks, and organize countermovements against them. But we don't have the right, without demonstrating a diseased intolerance, to tell them to stop trying to force their values on us.

My point is that the concept of tolerance has been misused and redefined in the current cultural debate to make even the attempt to persuade an act of intolerance. There are unethical (and ultimately unhelpful) ways of getting people to change their fundamental allegiances in life. These include coercion, deception, and bribery, and Christianity, along with various secular movements, has at times used each of these in its history.

> **My point is that the concept of tolerance has been misused and redefined in the current cultural debate to make even the attempt to persuade an act of intolerance.**

Coercion used to be thought of as burning at the stake, the threat of exile or excommunication, concentration camps, or the denial of a job or housing. It now has been redefined to include knocking on a neighbor's door, handing out a tract, or singing a Christmas carol in school. If someone else is telling you things you do not wish to hear, call it intolerance and you can both silence that person and maintain the moral high ground yourself. It's a neat trick if you can get away with it—and many people are doing just that.

Actually, one does not even have to try to change someone's mind to be considered intolerant, one only has to fail to affirm or to agree. In a new twist on the old saying, "If you are not for me, you are against me," we now have, "If you do not agree with me, you hate me." This is the case no matter how civil, reasonable, and reluctant your disagreement might be. And it has nothing to do with tolerance as it has traditionally been understood. Tolerance requires me to allow you your belief, it does not require me to endorse it. In fact, healthy tolerance allows me to argue forcefully against it—and it gives you the same right regarding me.

Those accused of intolerance are usually thought to be guilty of one of two supporting sins—ignorance or heartlessness. A newspaper article praising a documentary on gay activism on college campuses notes that some might fault the film for not including anyone who sees the homosexual lifestyle as "sinful," but then concludes, "Anyone who tried to make that argument after the poignant stories of Gary and others would look stupid or heartless or both."[3] Stupid or heartless—not much of a choice, but the only one afforded those out of step with the moral climate of our times.

There are many other slogans in the tolerance wars that one could analyze. The bumper sticker slogan "I tolerate everything except intolerance" is laughably circular in its reasoning, naive in its assumptions, and immoral if actually practiced. Does this person tolerate, for instance, the destruction of the environment or the starving of distant children—both of which result from greed or indifference, not from intolerance?

And, of course, there are the equally dubious counterslogans of some moral conservatives. The one that seems to come most easily to the lips is the slogan, "I hate the sin but love the sinner." It certainly expresses God's own attitude, but unless matched by actions, it is thoroughly unconvincing.

And then there are those who seem to feel that all they have to do to be righteous and victorious is to put an "anti-" prefix in front of any good thing—anti-God, anti-Bible, anti-family—and attach it to their enemies. We should be skeptical about such words not only because they are often unfairly applied, but also because they are designed to get people to react, not to think. For unreflective people, the label or slogan does all their thinking for them.

Slogans, however, are not the only useful strategy. Another is to attach one's own causes with other popular causes from the past or present that are more universally praised. It is common, for instance, to tie the campaign to legitimize homosexual behavior with past and ongoing efforts to win civil and other rights for African Americans and women. The argument goes something like this: "People of color and women were once denied many basic rights and freedoms by intolerant people. That intolerance was eventually overcome. Today some people continue to show their intolerance by opposing, for instance, gay marriage. In the same way that tolerance won out for African Americans and women, it ought to and will win out for homosexuals and lesbians."

This strategy is especially effective if one has already established a climate where tolerance is automatically a good thing and intolerance an automatic evil. It discourages people from asking inconvenient questions, such as whether all sexual behavior is as unambiguously and automatically a good or neutral thing as is race and gender. It is also rhetorically helpful if one confuses in people's minds two separate issues: whether gays have been badly treated (which they clearly have) with the separate issue of whether homosexual behavior is a good or healthy or morally neutral thing. It is easier to assert the acceptability of homosexual sex if people generally have been persuaded to associate any opposition to it with earlier opposition to the rights of minorities and women.

Tolerance and the Church

I would like to think that the charge of intolerance against morally conservative Christians is entirely wrongheaded, a badge to be worn proudly by a people committed to goodness and truth no matter what the cost. The problem is, I hang around church too much. I hear too many sermons, too many Christian gurus on the radio and television, and get too much Christian mail from too many Christian organizations. It's difficult to argue with a straight face that Christians are unfairly accused of intolerance when I so often see the very attitudes of diseased intolerance we have discussed: suspicion, mean-spiritedness, aggressive ignorance, close-mindedness, primitive anger, and refusal to dialogue.

The activists on both sides in the tolerance wars, in fact, look and sound a lot like each other. Consider the American Civil Liberties Union (ACLU), an organization as self-declaredly opposed to the social agenda of conservative Christianity as any. The tone of their fundraising letters, like most such appeals, is consistently alarmist, simplistic, and sarcastic. Consider the following representative declarations: "Freedom vs. authoritarianism. That's what the struggle over competing visions of mo-

> **The activists on both sides in the tolerance wars, in fact, look and sound a lot like each other.**

rality is all about." "Increasingly we are being as-
saulted with the belief that somehow we are a
nation in steep moral decline." "We are being
told by the *Merchants of Virtue* . . . that we should
return to those good old days." "Right now those
who would impose their pious standards of morality on private, personal behavior are danger-
ously close to winning the debate."[4] Not exactly
an appeal to sweet reason.

Surely Christians are different. Surely Christians speak to the sinner with a broken heart. In
many places perhaps, but not in my mailbox,
not on my radio. Consider the following ex-
cerpts from a fund-raising letter, typical of
those from many highly successful Christian
organizations: "these shameful 'high priests' of
the anti-virtue movement," "as God's people
for this historic hour, we rise to the challenge
and give whatever it takes to turn back the
anti-Christian juggernaut which threatens our
way of life," "Do not doubt that prayer will become a crime, the Bible off-limits, and sharing
our faith in public forbidden." Who can resist
reaching for his or her checkbook when the
whole cosmos is at stake?

The point is not the validity of the fund-raising letter's position. The point is that its tactics, as is so often the case in the culture wars, undermines its Christianity. It displays all the familiar manipulative strategies of modern advertising and political propaganda. The envelope even gives the false impression that it is a registered letter, a touch worthy of magazine subscription marketers and vacation scams. Winning is losing if this is how we are to win the culture wars.

Another problem for morally conservative Christians in easily shrugging off the charge of intolerance is what seems to many the selective nature of our moral outrage. We appear to be in a continual lather over things sexual—pornography, homosexuality, abortion, prostitution, adultery, sex education, promiscuity, and fornication—yet we have been amazingly patient, even lethargic, about the evils of racism, and positively resistant to righting the wrongs of sexism. The recent counterattack in the "values" sector of the culture wars, in fact, has the liberals shouting that they are the moral ones because they are fighting hunger, injustice, and the like, while conservatives are just interested in getting their long, blue noses into people's bedrooms.

Not surprising, then, that the public perception of conservative Christians in dealing with those with whom they disagree is somewhere to the right of Rasputin. They are seen as the pit bulls of the culture wars—small brains, big teeth, strong jaws, and no interest in compromise. Fair? Often not. Understandable? Absolutely.

One Woman's Day among the Christians

Most of this discussion has proceeded with abstract assertions bolstered by the occasional snippet of an example. Allow me to tell a story at some length that illustrates much of what we have been exploring as these issues work themselves out in the real world. I do not wish to offer a long litany of offenses—real or imagined—against conservative Christians and Christian values by hypocritical secularists.[5] I want to tell the story of a well-meaning, open, refreshingly honest woman who found herself at a convention for Christian counselors and didn't know what to make of it.

□ □

Mary Sykes Wylie is a self-described "liberal humanist" psychologist whose assignment is to attend the 1999 World Conference of the American Association of Christian Counselors. She is there to find out about this fringe group within her profession that believes it can combine contemporary psychotherapy with old-fashioned religion. And she is both attracted and repelled.[6]

Her first shock is when everyone starts singing, not a common practice at secular psychotherapy professional meetings. She asks herself, "What am I doing here?" and wonders whether she should pretend to sing along.

The next stunner is listening to the keynote speaker, Joni Eareckson Tada, well known to evangelicals, but a puzzling new voice for Mary. Tada asserts that the reason life is painful is so we will be forced to look for God. She speaks of the new body she will receive one day to replace the paralyzed body she has lived in since her diving accident decades ago.

Mary finds the talk offensive to her professionally, but somehow powerful at an affective level. She says she is embarrassed by the "manipulative pathos and manufactured spirituality" and yet finds Tada's hope for a new body "authentically heart-breaking." The talk awakens in her old yearnings for some kind of hope that death—"Nobody gets out alive"—is not the absolute end. She wonders if it is simply escapism or if there may be something to this "heart-pumping hope" that "whatever awfulness transpires in our lives," believers are part of a "glorious story that has only just begun."

Finding, however, that her emotions and longings are taking her places that her intellect does not want to go, she does something interesting and very relevant to our discussion of tolerance and intolerance. She reminds herself that the people she is with are the intolerant people, and that therefore they are not to be believed. Her lengthy explanation deserves to be in her own words:

> Still, it isn't a story I want in my life right at the moment, and I make myself remember the many good reasons it seems I have to dislike this particular plot line. I come to the conference sharing with other secular professionals a certain attitude about conservative evangelical

Christianity, based on a smorgasbord of impressions from the media, from chance acquaintances, from my own experience. I think of recent attempts to foist "creation science" on public schools; of radio preachers fulminating against gays, feminists, "New-Agers," Disney Studios, the ACLU and the United Nations; of the Southern Baptists commanding every wife to "submit herself graciously" to her husband, declaring Hindus and Muslims to be "lost in hopeless darkness" and calling for the conversion of Jews. More personally, I think of all the people I have cared about, who are apparently among these "lost souls"—a Jewish woman who has been a best friend since college, a beloved gay relative and her significant other now celebrating more than 25 years of life together, the Buddhist *sensei* who helped me experience the power of inner quietness, the science professor who humbled me with his discussion of geological time and the infinitesimally short blip of human presence at the tip of that awesome span. With these thoughts, it is not hard to work a good case against the Christian right. Ignorance, arrogance, self-righteousness, bigotry—there are more than enough examples among the fold to repel any self-respecting liberal humanist.

There are many elements at play here. She rightly sees that her own way of understanding the world is under threat. To defend the story she is now living against this new (yet old) threat, she forces herself to recall ("I make myself remember") why she and people like her do not like "conservative evangelical Christianity." She says she brings "a certain attitude" to the conference, but "attitude" in this case is a softer word for prejudice and stereotyping. She already knows what she is supposed to think of these people because of the group in which she has placed them.

She is honest enough to confess that this "attitude" is "based on a smorgasbord of impressions," as is usually the case with prejudice and intolerance. And it is not surprising that she identifies the media as the first source of her image of conservative Christians and "chance acquaintances" as her second. Presumably, this refers to brief encounters with conservative believers, though she doesn't cite any.

Her third category is telling. After listing many media-shaped controversies—from Darwin to Disney—that have colored her impressions, she moves to personal relationships. She doesn't give examples of being personally offended or of conservatives directly mistreating people she knows. Rather, she talks about friends and acquaintances who she believes would be hurt or made irrelevant if conservative Christians were to carry the day in our culture, and she sums up her impression of such people with the familiar words "ignorance, arrogance, self-righteousness, bigotry."

It is important to see that her opposition to what she perceives as conservative Christianity in action is personal, not intellectual (though she could undoubtedly muster arguments if pressed). It is at the personal level that the tolerance wars are won and lost. And it is at this level that conservative Christians are widely perceived to be losing (recall the newspaper article that dismissed anyone who thought homosexual practice wrong as "stupid or heartless or both").

Neither Mary nor the newspaper article, which could be multiplied thousands of times, presents any logical arguments for seeing homosexual behavior as healthy and whole. They can assume it is so because they have shown that the particular gay people in question are kind, appealing, and "beloved." The failure to affirm such people is, self-evidently, intolerant and itself blameworthy.

Mary can rightly be criticized for resorting to stereotypes and prejudice in an effort to defend against stereotypes and prejudice. Only *some* conservatives are hateful to gays, only *some* Christians are arrogantly dismissive of other people's religious beliefs, only *some* who believe in a Creator believe the world is only six thousand years old. Only some.

Only some, I say. But then again, too many. If Mary is honest enough to admit that the Christian story might have something she needs, shouldn't I be honest enough to confess that I and others are sometimes infected with things she is right to condemn? Can I really proclaim that I *haven't* seen ignorance, arrogance, self-righteousness, and bigotry in my own subculture and my own life? Is it enough to comfort myself with the truth that there is just as much of it in Mary's liberal secularist subculture? Is it clear which of us has the mote in our eye and which the beam? Is *any* moral failure, including my own, merely a mote to God?

Mary's story is not over. She does an extraordinary thing. After retreating into the protection of stereotypes about hateful and narrow conservative Christians, she admits, "none of *those* Christians seem to be at *this* meeting." She is forced to admit that these *particular* Christians seem more or less acceptable, though with a disturbing penchant for talking about sin. She finds the "harshness" of the concept of sin mitigated by an atmosphere of compassion and love. In short, she experiences the best antidote for much, though not all, intolerance—actual, personal contact with individuals from the objectionable group.

> **She is forced to admit that these *particular* Christians seem more or less acceptable, though with a disturbing penchant for talking about sin.**

Is Mary's experience an example of intolerance from those who most champion tolerance? I don't think so. She flirts with it, is tempted by it, but finally overcomes it. If tolerance is putting up with the objectionable, she finally decides to put up with these strange Christians. She is defensive, a bit judgmental perhaps, but she gives them a hearing and even admits they *may* have something to offer her: "The words I hear at this conference and afterward glimmer with implicit promises that are hard to resist—the promise of freedom from the chronic anxiety that we will never be quite attractive, smart or successful enough; the promise of relief from exhausting obsession with our own tiny, earthbound, egocentric selves; the promise of unconditional love in spite of the deep-down suspicion that we are really pretty unlovable." It requires quite a bit of courage, in fact, as well as tolerance, for her to publish such an honest account in a professional journal. It cannot have been well received by everyone, and I admire her for her pluck.

Are we as honest and courageous as Mary? Many morally conservative Christians are—ready to acknowledge what they have learned from those who do not share their core convictions, eager to be channels for healing and compassion rather than for anger and condemnation, ready to listen as well as to speak. But others are not, and most of us are somewhere in between. We struggle to identify that line between compassion and enabling, between humility and enfeebling relativism, between healthy tolerance and moral paralysis.

Both Compassion *and* Truth:
The Need for a Moral Community

The insistence on an uncritical tolerance is a call for compassion at the expense of truth. The response is too often an angry call for truth at the expense of compassion. The twin extremes of authoritarianism and relativism are both an offense against wholeness. Both harm individuals and communities. Both seize partial truths and declare them as though they were whole truths.

The twin extremes of authoritarianism and relativism are both an offense against wholeness.

And both are embraced by people with good motives who genuinely want the world to be a better place.

Pascal said, "Men never do evil so fully and cheerfully as when we do it out of conscience." Most tolerance-wars activists are, in fact, people of conscience. Each side is sure the world is sliding into a moral cesspool and only people like themselves stand in the way. Each side has its favorite horror stories—the Inquisition and McCarthyism on one hand, deadly political, social, and sexual revolutions on the other.

Inquisitions and revolutions, however, are perhaps overly dramatic examples of the dangers we are talking about. More trees rot in the forest than are destroyed by fire. Societies more often decay than explode. And both intolerant authoritarianism and overly tolerant relativism are signs of decay.

And both are also obstacles to the maintenance of a crucially needed moral community. A moral community is the collective will in a society to value and protect the good, the true, and the just. It requires the moral confidence that these are real and knowable things, and the moral courage to act.

Is there a moral community left in our relativistic world? That is an important question deserving careful discussion. Perhaps only fragments of one are left. Certainly there are things that all people of goodwill agree on. We can work to expand these areas of agreement, laboring for a just and truthful society, even as we refuse to abandon our defining convictions.

4 Tolerance and the Bible: How Tolerant Is God?

I believe that unarmed truth and unconditional love will have the final word in reality. That is why right, temporarily defeated, is stronger than evil triumphant.

MARTIN LUTHER KING JR.

As People of the Book, conservative Christians usually ask, "What does the Bible say?" Well, what *does* the Bible say about tolerance? Is God tolerant? Ought we to be?

There are actually three different relationships in the Bible that reveal something about the question of tolerance: the relationship between God and humanity, especially his relationships with believers; the relationship of believer to believer within the believing community; and the relationship between the believing community and other people and cultures.

Consider first the general relationship of God to humanity, especially to believers. Asking whether God is tolerant is a bit like asking whether Ahab's pursuit of Moby Dick is a violation of the Endangered Species Act. The question is inadequately framed. God is simultaneously tolerant, intolerant, and far beyond the category of tolerance.

The Bible certainly teaches us that God hates sin. That much is clear. He is depicted as morally uncompromising, righteously angry, holy, and sure to punish evil. In our own culture, that is enough in itself to earn God the label of intolerant.

Yet he is also depicted as patient, long-suffering, forgiving, and slow to anger—all qualities associated with tolerance. It seems he does, in a sense, tolerate sin—at least for a season. If tolerance is putting up with the objectionable and withholding the power to coerce conformity with one's own views, then it seems God is certainly tolerant of us. We do much that displeases him, that violates who he is and what he made us to be, and yet he does not immediately destroy us or even force us into obedience.

Consider the first time God chooses to reveal his character—his essential nature—to the people of Israel. He is speaking to Moses at the time of the giving of the Ten Commandments (Exodus 34:67):

The Lord passed in front of Moses, calling out,

> "The Lord! The Lord!
>   The God of compassion and mercy!
> I am slow to anger
>   and rich in unfailing love and faithfulness.
> I lavish unfailing love to a thousand generations.
>   I forgive iniquity, rebellion, and sin.
> But I do not excuse the guilty.
>   I punish the children and grandchildren
> for the sins of their parents
>   to the third and fourth generations."

The very first thing God wishes to proclaim about himself to Israel is that he is merciful, gracious, slow to anger, and overflowing with love and faithfulness. These qualities make mere tolerance look pale and cold in comparison.

This declaration is immediately followed by— or fused with—the balancing proclamation that he judges the guilty and that the consequences of sin fall even on those around the guilty person. The latter seems unfair to the modern, individualistic sensibility, but we have only to look at the consequences of sin within households and over

generations to see that this declaration has more
to do with the spreading effects of sin than it does
the vengefulness of God.

If we can't understand the "But" (v. 7) resting
between love and judgment, we can never understand God's character or our own status before him.
We will tend always to fall either into the pit of self-
loathing or the pit of self-pity, believing we are un-
worthy of God's mercy or undeserving of God's
judgment. We will reshape the complex wholeness
of God's character into the simplistic cartoons of
cheap grace or lightning-bolt destroyer.

The Old Testament abounds with descriptions
and images and stories of God that emphasize this
balance between love and judgment. In Psalm
103 we find the following:

> The Lord is merciful and gracious,
>   slow to get angry and full of unfailing love.
> He will not constantly accuse us,
>   nor remain angry forever.
> He does not punish us for all our sins;
>   he does not deal harshly with us, as we deserve.
> For his unfailing love toward those who fear him
>   is as great as the height of the heavens above
>   the earth.

He has removed our sins as far from us
   as the east is from the west.
The Lord is like a father to his children,
   tender and compassionate to those who
      fear him.
For he knows how weak we are;
   he remembers we are only dust. (vv. 8-14)

Again, this is love, not just tolerance, but notice that there *is* something to which to object. The psalmist acknowledges our collective sins. God has just *reason* to punish us. But he chooses instead to be merciful and gracious. This overlaps slightly with the idea of tolerance, but it is so much more than merely "putting up with." It is grace and love.

This mercy and grace and love, however, is not based on, and does not result in, ignoring or treating lightly the sin that makes them necessary. God does not affirm us in our sin, nor is he indifferent to our sin. He loves us despite our sin. And that love does not even mean we will escape the consequences of our sin, including, at times, God's punishment. It does mean, however, that at no point does God withdraw his love from us.

This attitude and action of God is instructive to us as we try to figure out our relation to a fallen culture. As believers, we are not only receivers of love and mercy, we are also to be givers of love and mercy. It is not so much *our* love and mercy that we give, because we have a very limited capacity for either. But we can be conduits for God's love and mercy to others. In being that conduit, we should not compromise God's character by pretending that his love winks at evil, individual or collective. We have no right to offer cheap and easy grace where there is no repentance or desire for forgiveness and change.

God does not affirm us in our sin, nor is he indifferent to our sin. He loves us despite our sin.

But neither do we have the right to pick and choose whom God will love and forgive. We are foolish not to understand that our sins are no less grievous and offensive to God than the sins of those who most offend us. The Bible is replete with examples of God dealing more harshly with the sins of those who call on his name than with those who do not acknowledge him.

Tolerance among Believers:
The Quest for Shalom

The Bible also speaks often to the second relationship in which tolerance is a factor—that between believers within the faith community. In the Old Testament large sections are devoted to describing and prescribing how the people of Israel should relate to each other. These are often in the form of legal, economic, and social expectations, but they are not merely dry, mechanical formulas. They are practical manifestations and applications in law and custom of the same love and justice that has been part of God's revealed character from the beginning.

The goal of the relationships of God to his people and his people with each other is shalom. Shalom, in fact, is what God intends for the entire world. It is the goal toward which all our efforts should point. Though it is a much different and more profound concept than tolerance, it can help us think more clearly about when and how we should be tolerant and when and why we should not.

What is *shalom*? It is a Hebrew word for a concept that is nothing less than God's vision for his entire creation, especially as it manifests itself in human well-being: individual, interpersonal, and social. *Shalom* appears more than 250 times in the Old Testament and many times more in its Greek counterpart *(eirene)* in the New Testament. It means so many different but related things that it is difficult to know where to begin in trying to understand it.

The definition most people know is peace. The peace of shalom, however, is much more than the absence of war or of conflict. It is the peace that comes from everything being right in the world, each thing and person in its proper place doing that which it was created to do. (Of course, if you do not believe there is any such thing as "proper" or "created" then you will not believe in or seek shalom.)

Shalom can have all the following meanings in the Bible depending on the context: completeness, friendship, well-being, prosperity, health, contentedness, safety, and even salvation. It includes the sense of nothing lacking, nothing out of balance. It is associated with order and law and judgment—political and divine. Crucially for our consideration of tolerance, shalom is

> **It is the peace that comes from everything being right in the world, each thing and person in its proper place doing that which it was created to do.**

also associated with righteousness. An offense against God's righteousness is an offense against shalom, an offense that harms both the individual and the community.

Shalom in the Bible is not the product of human effort, though humans can destroy it. Shalom is the gift of God, and it can be taken away by God (as the prophets warn). In the New Testament Christ is seen as the bringer of shalom, restoring in the kingdom all right relationships, and Satan is continually trying to destroy shalom.

Shalom is not only God's intention for us, it is evidence of his love for us. This love is reflected in his compassion and grace but also in his laws and commands. God insists on obedience to his law not because he is a petty tyrant but because, as the one who made us, he knows what is necessary for us to thrive. Moral commands are God's love in the form of law. This is difficult to understand for those steeped in individualism and relativism.

Wholeness and well-being are the essence of shalom. Brokenness and disease (dis-ease) result when shalom is ruptured. The statement "God is in his heaven, and all is right with the world" is a declaration of shalom. And no offense to shalom can ever be purely personal, because any disruption of shalom harms everyone.

Understanding shalom provides a paradigm for understanding how Christians should conduct themselves in regard to present-day calls for tolerance. It also helps us understand the recurring New Testament concern for relationships between believers. If Christians cannot achieve shalom among themselves, then the witness of the gospel is blunted.

The New Testament echoes the Old Testament balance of God's righteousness and God's grace that we saw earlier. And just as the Old Testament is concerned with how people treat each other within the nation of Israel, so the New Testament repeatedly focuses on how believers are to treat each other within the church. To the extent that tolerance is an issue in the New Testament, it is more often a question of Christians needing to learn to get along with *each other* than it is a question of how believers relate to a pagan culture.

That requirement to get along is not merely pragmatism or a call to be nice. It is rooted, as in the Old Testament, in the character of God and in his saving work through the Incarnation.

Consider, for instance, chapter 14 and the beginning of chapter 15 of Romans. This is the "weaker brother" passage that speaks to both sides in a disagreement among believers regarding any matter of conscience. Paul tells the person whose conscience is bothered by a certain behavior not to act judgmentally toward a fellow believer whose conscience is not bothered. But he also tells the second believer not to insist on his right to do what his conscience allows if that behavior disrupts the well-being of the first believer—thereby threatening the shalom of the community.

> **T**olerance in the New Testament is more often a question of Christians needing to learn to get along with *each other* than it is a question of how believers relate to a pagan culture.

Paul rejects the radical individualism common to our own time that makes an absolute out of individual rights: "We don't live for ourselves or die for ourselves." Paul says instead that we live and die to the Lord. And from this he draws a conclusion: We should quit passing judgment on each other, realizing that "we will all stand before the judgment seat of God." Instead we must learn to live in peace and "aim for harmony in the church and try to build each other up."

Paul continues by linking community harmony with the work of Christ, culminating in chapter 15 verse 7: "Accept each other just as Christ has accepted you so that God will be given glory." Just as Christ accepted us, despite our unworthiness, we should accept one another, whether deserved or not. Getting along with each other requires extending to others, on a small scale, the overwhelming grace that was first extended to us by Christ. And we are to do this not simply because it is right and will make things easier for us, but because it will bring deserved praise to God, in whom the grace originated.

The call for believers to live in peace with each other is repeated throughout the New Testament. Paul often specifies the particular attitudes and actions that are necessary. One such passage is found in Romans 12. It includes things such as self-sacrifice, encouragement, generosity, kindness, honor, joy, hope, patience, hospitality, harmony, and humility. The whole is summed up in the command to genuinely love each other, in action not just in word.

Similar passages appear in 2 Corinthians 6, Galatians 5, Ephesians 4, and Colossians 3. Part of the Colossians passage reads as follows:

> Since God chose you to be the holy people he loves, you must clothe yourselves with tenderhearted mercy, kindness, humility, gentleness, and patience. Make allowance for each other's faults and forgive anyone who offends you. Remember, the Lord forgave you, so you must forgive others. Above all, clothe yourselves with love, which binds us all together in perfect harmony. (vv. 12-14)

In older translations, "make allowance" is rendered "bear with." Note how similar "bear with one another" is to the "bear with" meaning of the Latin word which is the root for our English word *tolerance*. Although the Bible calls us to attitudes and actions that are far beyond mere tolerance, there is also a fair amount of simple "putting up with" that is required in any family or community or human gathering, whether of faith or otherwise.

Paul is very realistic about this. He has lived among people of faith and among pagans. He knows the twistedness of his own heart. He therefore knows that wherever two or three are gathered together, there is fallenness—and the potential for conflict.

He also knows how important it is that believers do, in fact, get along. A spirit of peace and mutual support is a crucial evidence of the truth of faith. As such, it is also a key witness to those outside the faith. If believers "are always biting and devouring one another" (Gal. 5:15), why should anyone else want to be one of them? This was a painful question for the church in Paul's time that continues to this day.

It is clear, however, that tolerance is not enough. "Putting up with" is the minimum requirement for superficial social peace. It is good and necessary, but it is not adequate to establish the kind of shalom that the kingdom of God requires. Paul underscores this when he follows the "bear with" command with another command: "Above all, clothe yourselves with love, which binds us all together in perfect harmony" (Col. 3:14). Love is the overarching force of which the particular virtues are specific manifestations. Love makes possible and gives power to compassion, patience, forgiveness, and all the rest.

Elsewhere Paul makes it clear that believers

should also seek shalom with the culture at large. In Romans, for instance, he says, "Never pay back evil with more evil. Do things in such a way that everyone can see you are honorable. Do all that you can to live in peace with everyone" (12:17-18). Shalom, he tells us, is so valuable that we should go so far as to "bless those who persecute you" (v. 14) in order not to disrupt it.

Clearly intolerance within the body of believers in the New Testament is the enemy of shalom. It usually arises from some form of pride or feeling of superiority or competition. Though the intolerant often appeal to God's law or to righteousness as the basis for their position, the unloving spirit of their behavior betrays their own self-centered motives and stubbornness.

Paul's call for peace within the community, however, is never at the cost of holiness or righteousness. There is no "Who am I to say?" in Paul—or any other biblical writer—when it comes to those who disrupt the community with persistent sinning. He particularly hates *arrogant* sinning. A case of incest within the church in Corinth causes him to write that even the pagans don't approve of such things, yet the Corinthians foolishly congratulate themselves on their tolerance. "You are so proud of yourselves, but you should be mourning in sorrow and shame" (1 Cor. 5:2). Even though he is not in Corinth, he feels free to be intolerant of this behavior: "I have already passed judgment on this man in the name of the Lord Jesus" (1 Cor. 5:3-4). He believes he knows sin when he sees it and is responsible to name it and deal with it. This is one reason Paul is unpopular in some Christian circles today. He is so loving at one time and so, well, intolerant at another.

Our contemporary training in tolerance encourages us to feel it is "not our business" when someone else among the believers falls into sin. At most the church leaders are responsible to deal with it, but even they are likely to be reluctant or told to mind their own business.

There is, however, no *private* sin in the New Testament church. Private sin creates a community problem. Sin must be taken seriously because it is the enemy of all God wants to do in the world. No healthy understanding of tolerance will explain away sin, evil, or brokenness.

Paul takes sin seriously, but he takes forgiveness even more so. He calls for the man who committed incest to be handed over to Satan—

hardly, it would seem, a loving thing to do. But the purpose is not for punishment for its own sake, but so that the man, perhaps because he will be so miserable, will repent and "he himself will be saved on the day the Lord returns" (1 Cor. 5:5).

Paul regularly blasts away at unrepentant and arrogant sin but counsels grace and restoration for those who seek forgiveness. The *attitude* of a person toward his or her sin is crucial. Later Paul tells the Corinthians that they should forgive and comfort a man who had repented of a sin that seriously affected the community of believers: "It is time to forgive him and comfort him. Otherwise he may become so discouraged that he won't be able to recover. Now show him that you still love him" (2 Cor. 2:7-8). This clearly is not mere tolerance; it is restorative forgiveness and love.

So is Paul or the Bible generally, as some have suggested, intolerant? Only in the sense that we all should be. God hates that which destroys shalom within the church and promotes suffering within the world.

God hates that which destroys shalom within the Church and promotes suffering within the world.

Tolerance in Relation to the World

We have looked briefly at the question of tolerance in the relationships of God to humanity and
of believer to believer. What does the Bible suggest about tolerance in that third relationship, the
one between believers and the larger world? How
tolerant is God of a fallen world and how tolerant
should we be?

As complex as this question is, I am tempted to
begin and end with a simple biblical assertion that
every Christian knows. Because it is so encompass-
ing and because it explains so much, it is one of the
first verses believers teach their children: "For
God loved the world so much that he gave his only
Son, so that everyone who believes in him will not
perish but have eternal life" (John 3:16).

Any view of God's relationship to human culture and to men and women outside the faith that
does not start with God's love has started at the
wrong point. God's love is the master theme of
creation, and no amount of sin and brokenness
can erase it. And it provides the essential model
for how believers are to relate to a fallen world.

Such talk sometimes makes nervous those believers who fear that speaking about God's love will

be separated from speaking about God's justice, re-sulting in a watery, self-esteem theology that soft-pedals sin and encourages accommodation with an evil society. Some have done exactly that, but such a separation betrays a failure to understand that love and justice are in fact inseparable.

There is nothing weak about God's love and nothing harsh about God's justice. His love is not weak because it is the power that made the uni-verse and it allows people to endure every kind of suffering under the sun with courage and hope. His justice is not harsh precisely because it is itself an expression of that love and therefore works only to bring us and the world back to wholeness. True harshness is the encouragement of or indif-ference to the sin in the world that keeps people from the state of shalom that God intends.

The Bible, then, establishes love, not tolerance, as the standard by which we are to relate to all people—both within and without the community of believers. That call to love is not based on the lovableness of the one to be loved. Certainly God did not wait for us to be lovable before he loved us: "God showed his great love for us by sending Christ to die for us while we were still sinners" (Romans 5:8). The "while we were still sinners" is crucial. An intolerant God would destroy us in our sin. A tolerant God would merely put up with our sin. A loving God dies for our sin.

This loving God reaches out for a relationship with us, offering forgiveness and healing. It is not done grudgingly or condescendingly or judgmentally. It is offered by One who has the authority to do so, based on the rights of the Creator over creation and on the character of a God whose essence is goodness, justice, compassion, mercy, and holiness. (It is an offer, however, that we are allowed to refuse.)

An intolerant God would destroy us in our sin. A tolerant God would merely put up with our sin. A loving God dies for our sin.

Christ dying for us, as the ultimate expression of God's love for us while we were yet sinners, is the model for the relationship of believers to an unbelieving world. It is the goal we espouse when we seek to "hate the sin but love the sinner." But it is a goal we too often fail to reach. Many times when we see what we know to be evil in the world, we see an enemy to be defeated rather than someone broken to be healed. We make an initial show of compassion, but when rebuffed turn quickly to anger and condemnation.

This is not the model Christ offers us. Consider Zacchaeus (Luke 19). Zacchaeus was a cheater and an oppressor. As the chief tax collector for his region, he had to wring from the people the tax demanded by Rome and then squeeze out as much more as he could for himself. He was the lowest of the low in the eyes of his fellow Jews.

And he was also the fellow Jesus wanted to have dinner with. Jesus did not wait for Zacchaeus to seek him out. He did not wait for him to feel bad about his sins, much less repent of them. He also did not attack him for his sin, as it would seem any good person should do. Instead, he honored him—by giving him the opportunity to receive him in Zacchaeus's own home.

Predictably, the crowd did not like it: " 'He has gone to be the guest of a notorious sinner,' they grumbled" (Luke 19:7). You and I wouldn't have liked it either, and we shouldn't pretend otherwise. It is as though a great and godly Christian leader is coming to your church. The church has been cleaned and decorated. There is a full schedule of meetings and services, and a sold-out banquet to honor the leader. As he gets out of his car, he is greeted by local pastors amidst a swarm of admirers and people who want to get a glimpse of the famous and respected man.

But protesters are also there because of the public stand the man has taken on controversial social issues. Among the protestors is the leader of the local gay activists, holding a sign condemning the Christian leader as an intolerant bigot. Some of the church people are angry that the man is here with his sign and are trying to screen him from view.

As the Christian leader goes up the steps of the church, he sees the man and his sign and pauses. Pulling away from those who are ushering him into the church, he goes over to the activist with the sign and says, "I must stay at your house today." He takes the man back to his car and they drive away, leaving the schedule in tatters and his hosts gaping. Do you imagine them to be happy? Or yourself if you were on the planning committee?

The analogy is imperfect but I think helpful. It is so easy to affirm biblical stories and so difficult to live them out in our own lives and time. And what happens in the biblical story? Zacchaeus is the one who brings up his sin, not Jesus.

Zacchaeus is eager to repent and make restitution. Notice that Jesus neither denies Zacchaeus's sin nor tries to minimize or explain it away. Jesus accepts the repentance and proposed restitution, and welcomes Zacchaeus back into the community: "Salvation has come to this home today, for this man has shown himself to be a true son of Abraham" (Luke 19:9). In accepting Zacchaeus's restitution and welcoming him back into the community, Jesus is repairing shalom.

Would this happen today with an angry gay activist? Have we tried? Would the rejection of a loving offer prove it was wrong to have made the offer? How many times should we be willing to be rejected—perhaps seventy times seven?

Tolerance and Being a Neighbor

Or consider the story of the Good Samaritan. Jesus tells this story after acknowledging the centrality of the command to love our neighbors as ourselves and then being asked to define "neighbor" (see Luke 10:30-37). We all know that in the story the religious and respectable people fail the test of neighborliness, which is part of the larger test of shalom. We also all know that the Samaritans were despised by the Jews and that Jesus uses a Samaritan as the hero to challenge his listeners' assumptions.

What makes the Samaritan a model of neighborliness, and what might we learn from him about tolerance? To begin with, he does not evaluate the worth or social status of the one who needs help. He does not ask whether it is a fellow Samaritan or a Jew. Neither does he ask whether the victim is a good person, someone deserving of rescuing, or perhaps someone who has been up to no good and gotten exactly what he deserves. All he sees is a man in need of help and no one else to help him.

And of what does his help consist? He does not give him advice—"You ought to have somebody take a look at those cuts, buddy." He does not give him a moral lecture—"Don't you know it's stupid to travel alone on a road like this?" Instead, he personally tends to his wounds and pays for his extended care out of his own pocket, promising to keep in personal contact over time.

Again, put this too familiar story in a contemporary context. The man on the road has AIDS, perhaps in the early 1990s when the disease seemed likely to be an unstoppable plague and the fear of it was overpowering (which is still the

case in many parts of the world). Who is the priest in this new context? Who is the Levite? Who is the Samaritan? I will let you speak for yourself, but I find little in the story to give me comfort about my own neighborliness.

What does the story tell us about tolerance and love? It tells us we have a responsibility even to people we don't know (compare this with Jesus' reminder in Matthew 5 that there is no credit in acting lovingly toward those who already love you). It tells us that our primary attitude toward our neighbor should be concern for our neighbor's well-being—for shalom. Further it tells us this concern is not abstract and at a distance but is personal, involves both time and money, and extends beyond single encounters. It also tells us that none of this depends upon our neighbor deserving help, any more than God's love for us depends on our own merit.

What, similarly, does this story *not* tells us? It does not tell us that helping our neighbor requires us to affirm our neighbor's way of life. It does not tell us that we should make our neighbor feel good about his or her choices, or that the point of being a neighbor is to enhance others' self-esteem.

As so often in the Bible, we are called to hold two different but complementary ideas in tension together. Jesus' story of the Good Samaritan has been prompted by dual commands, found in varied forms in the Old Testament and the Gospels: " 'You must love the Lord your God with all your heart, all your soul, all your strength, and all your mind.' And, 'Love your neighbor as yourself' " (Luke 10:27). Too often these commands are taken separately and distorted in defense of judgmentalism on the one hand or moral passivity on the other. "Love the Lord your God" is used as a rationale for condemning people for their sinfulness, and "Love your neighbor" is distorted into a call for accepting sinful and destructive behavior. In one case, love is used as an excuse for condemning, in the other as an excuse for enabling.

Instead, we are called not to choose between these commands but to fuse them together. We show love for God *and* for our neighbor by the act of upholding God's law. Bringing God's law into the life of a broken neighbor is honoring to God and healing to the neighbor. But it will only be so if we have the untainted motives of the Good Samaritan.

Tolerance and Moral Failure

It is instructive that we find ourselves turning to stories to understand what the Bible has to say about love and tolerance and righteousness. Stories move us away from theory to the everyday world in which we must live. They give abstract principles the feel of flesh and blood, and help us feel the agony of difficult choices.

Perhaps the single most enlightening story for thinking about God's attitude toward tolerance is the Gospel story of the woman caught in adultery (John 8). We have in this ancient text all the elements of a contemporary "values clarification" exercise on tolerance: a woman accused of a sexual sin (her co-sinner nowhere to be seen), religious leaders insisting on strict application of the traditional moral law, and a crowd representing society as a whole. And we also have Jesus.

The religious leaders care less about the moral law, of course, than they do about defeating an enemy. (Sound familiar?) They have brought this woman to Jesus to trap him. Either he will deny the law of Moses and thereby lose his authority as a moral teacher, or he will agree to the condemnation of the woman and thereby lose the sympathy of the common people who chafe under the arrogant legalism of the religious leaders. (And he may also perhaps get himself in trouble with the Roman authorities, who alone can approve the death penalty.)

What would today's apostles of tolerance do? Point out, of course, that the woman and presumably her sexual partner are consenting adults. Who's to say that adultery is a sin? Whose business is it anyway? Perhaps it's of interest to any offended spouses but certainly not anyone else. The woman should be freed without blame, perhaps even commended for her bold defiance of archaic and sexist sexual norms, and directed to the nearest lawyer to discuss the merits of a lawsuit for harassment against her accusers.

What might today's public defenders of morality do? They would likely do about what the religious authorities of that day did. They would use the woman as a public example of sin, show little or no regard for her as a person, call for her public shaming, and use the whole situation to advance their call for a return to traditional morality. She would be the poster girl for their next fund-raising letter decrying the decline of religious values and calling for sacrificial financial support so that their organization could carry on God's fight against evil.

What does Jesus do? He does the seemingly impossible, affirming the moral law and at the same time refusing to humiliate the one against whom it is brought. He tells the religious leaders that the one of them who is without sin should cast the first stone (one cheer from lovers of tolerance). He then tells her that he does not condemn her (two cheers). But then, crucially, he says what no modern champion of tolerance is likely to say—"Go and sin no more" (a disappointed groan).

Jesus does not dismiss her sin, nor does he dismiss her. He calls her sin what it is, tacitly offers her forgiveness for it, and directs her to turn from sin in the future. This is neither tolerance nor intolerance; it is speaking the truth in love.

> **Jesus does not dismiss her sin, nor does he dismiss her.**

"Speak the truth in love" (Eph. 4:15)—a profound New Testament admonition that we dare not debase into another slogan. The first casualty of relativistic tolerance is truth. The first casualty of legalistic morality is love. The one who can hold on to both at the same time is a true follower of Jesus.

God does not call us to be tolerant of our neighbors. God calls us to love them—at least as much as we love ourselves. Ultimately, tolerance is too weak a concept to be attributed to God. God is so much more than tolerant that Christians can rightfully ignore it as a fundamental goal for their own lives—but only if they are willing to live by a much higher standard.

The conclusion that love is the central principle of the Bible, as it is of creation, is not surprising. Nor is it surprising that love is a far more profound and appropriate concept for governing human relations than is tolerance. But people of faith should not take too much comfort. It is one thing to invoke the principle of love—it is something else to live it.

We must be more convincing in showing that we love those whose sin we oppose. We must find better ways to demonstrate that we do, in fact, love the sinner while we hate the sin. Our response to abortion is instructive.

In the initial years after its legalization, religious opponents of abortion were widely accused of caring about the fetus but not about the woman or even the newborn child if the child was not aborted. It was easier to say abortion is a sin than to provide practical help to sinners. Since that time, countless programs, many of them volunteer, have arisen that minister to every need—physical, psychological, financial, and spiritual—of pregnant women in difficult circumstances. Tangible love has replaced empty denunciation.

We have failed so far to respond as well to homosexuals. We have not been on the front line in the fight against AIDS, just as we were not in the struggle against racism. How differently would conservative Christianity be perceived today if we had been the first and most passionate of those offering practical help to AIDS sufferers? Much of our response—verbal and nonverbal, literal and symbolic—suggests that we have a visceral disgust for the homosexual. It would not be hard for an observer to deduce that we hate the sinner every bit as much as the sin. We can say it isn't so, but talk is cheap. We do not have to affirm homosexuals in their homosexuality, as our culture insists, but we do have to love them, and we haven't yet figured out quite how to show that.

Will showing love to those who are broken *work?* Probably not on the public relations level. The Catholic Church *did* offer early, practical help to those suffering with AIDS, and its reward in New York was the Gay Pride Parade stopping in front of St. Patrick's Cathedral to mock and blaspheme. Correct a fool, Proverbs tells us, and the fool will hate you. (And what if *I* am the fool?)

□ □ □ □ □ □ □ □ □ □ □ □ □ □ □ □ □ □ □ □

Biblical love is always sacrificial love. The paradigm, again, is Christ: "God showed his great love for us by sending Christ to die for us while we were still sinners" (Romans 5:8). Don't say you love someone unless you are willing to suffer for him or her. Sacrificial love does not say, "Do as I do or you are going to hell." It says, "I would rather be crucified than have you be harmed."

We do not have to affirm homosexuals in their homosexuality, as our culture insists, but we do have to love them, and we haven't yet figured out quite how to show that.

Is God tolerant? Yes, more so than we are. But also less so. God's forbearance never compromises his holiness or justice. He forgives and waits where we attack and destroy. He grieves and judges where we are lax and indifferent. Our goal is to be as tolerant as God but not more so, praying earnestly for his discernment.

5 Practical Suggestions, Guidelines, and Principles

If only it were all so simple! If only there were evil people somewhere committing evil deeds, and it were necessary only to separate them from the rest of us and destroy them. But the line dividing good and evil cuts through the heart of every human being. And who is willing to destroy a piece of his own heart?

ALEKSANDR SOLZHENITSYN, *THE GULAG ARCHIPELAGO*

Tolerance originally was an issue of religion, now it has become almost a religion in itself. The question of how one should respond to the omnipresent calls for tolerance is not only an intellectual and theological one, but also very practical—and calls for a practical, everyday-world response. How are we to think? What are we to say? How are we to act?

What follows are questions and guide-

> The question of how one should respond to the omnipresent calls for tolerance is not only an intellectual and theological one, but also very practical.

lines and principles that grow out of our overall discussion of tolerance. They will not tell you exactly what to believe or do in every circumstance, but it is hoped they will help you think, feel, and act more clearly and truthfully.

Questions to Ask

Here are a series of questions one can ask in any situation in which tolerance is being invoked. The questions are grouped under *thinking,* on the one hand, and *speaking* and *acting* on the other.

THINKING

1. Is the concept of tolerance in this case being used correctly, in the sense of "putting up with the objectionable," or is it being misused to mean "affirming the diverse"?

2. Am I genuinely being asked to be *tolerant,* or am I being asked to *affirm* something I believe is wrong?

3. Is the tolerance being asked of me a healthy or diseased form of tolerance? Is it based on truth and compassion or on relativism and moral confusion?

4. Am I thinking clearly, or am I simply reacting? Am I carefully and prayerfully

weighing things, or am I being shaped by slogans and emotional appeals from either side? Am I seeking truth and goodness or merely defending my own ideology and narrow experience? Do I defend traditional morality simply because it's traditional or, on the other hand, abandon traditional morality simply because it's out of fashion?

5. What moral values are at stake? What truths? Is anything else at stake?

6. Does the Bible speak to this situation? Does it speak directly or indirectly? clearly or obscurely? Have I rightly understood the context of the relevant biblical passages and how that context might affect any present-day application?

7. Are there other faith traditions and other interpretations of relevant biblical passages that I must consider and respect— ones that cause other equally committed people of faith to see things differently than I do? Do our differences affect my response or not?

8. Has the church in the past dealt with this or similar issues? What can I learn from the

church's past experience? Where has it failed and where has it been faithful?

9. Who has written or spoken insightfully on these issues—from the past or present? What resources are available to me as I try to think this through?

SPEAKING AND ACTING

1. If I find that I cannot affirm or be indifferent to something, should I tolerate it or not?

2. If I decide I should tolerate it, what form should my tolerance take and to what degree should I tolerate it? What are the limits to my tolerance?

3. If I decide I should not tolerate something, what form should my intolerance take? What are the limits to my intolerance?

4. In both my speech and actions (realizing that speech is a form of action), what tone or attitude do I convey to those around me? Am I principled or arbitrary? Am I irenic (shalom loving) or combative?

5. Even when I base my response on a legitimate moral principle or biblical position, do I undercut it with a judgmental, unlov-

ing spirit? When I am accused of being intolerant, is it because I am a saint or because I am a jerk?

6. Do my thoughts, words, and actions flow out of God's love or out of my own anger and insecurity? Do I reflect God's ability to reject the sin and love the sinner?

7. Am I too narrow in my moral objections? Do I eagerly reject one set of sinful behaviors, while blind to or slow to reject another?

8. Am I sufficiently aware of the beam in my own eye as I point out the mote in someone else's eye?

9. Have I listened carefully and empathetically to the story of those I oppose?

10. Have I looked for ways to be compassionate even when I must be partially or wholly intolerant?

11. If others ask, "Who are you to say?" do I have an appropriate response?

12. Am I willing to pay a price for being considered intolerant? What price?

13. Am I willing to pay a price for being considered not tough enough on sin? What price?

14. Am I genuinely interested in the shalom—
    the well-being—of others and of society,
    or am I out to defeat my enemies?

GUIDELINES AND PRINCIPLES

These many questions could be joined by many
more. But they also could be reduced to one:
What would Jesus do? Try making this a serious
question and a guide for your life, not another
empty slogan. Consider the stories of Zacchaeus,
the woman at the well, the woman caught in
adultery, the cleansing of the temple, and many
others. These stories address moral issues not as
abstract puzzles but as concrete examples involv-
ing real consequences in real people's lives. What
do they teach us about the fusing of compassion
and truth?

What also do they teach us about the spirit in
which Jesus acted? Entailed in the question
"What would Jesus do?" is another question:
"How would Jesus do it?" The two questions are
inseparable. It is not enough to be right. We have
all heard someone assert something we believed
to be true but with such mean-spiritedness or arrogance that we cringed. The truth can be stran-
gled even by those who love it.

Morally conservative Christians have often been on the right side of controversial issues that touch on tolerance—from Wilberforce to Martin Luther King Jr. to Mother Teresa. But often we have not. The negative image of conservative Christians today is at least partly earned.

Why do Christians have such a difficult time being like Christ? Why, when we are confronted with sin, do we so often react with self-indulgent anger and condemnation? I believe we do so in part **The negative image of conservative Christians today is at least partly earned.** because we do not really trust the gospel. Turning the other cheek, the first shall be last, losing our life to gain it, loving our enemies. All these make for great sermons, but in our bones we appear not to believe they are practical for everyday living in a hostile society. We seem to believe instead that if we are not as aggressive and hardnosed as those who oppose us, then God (and our organization) will somehow be defeated and goodness will disappear from the earth. The result is that we are perceived, often not unfairly, as simply harsh, belligerent, and, yes, intolerant.

How *should* it be instead? How can we affirm

Christian morality, unapologetically rooted in the Bible, without becoming rhetorical bomb throwers? We cannot improve on the biblical command to "speak the truth in love." But we can try to flesh out some practial implications entailed in that command. We have done so throughout this discussion of tolerance, and here are two others.

First, we should resist any appeal whose primary aim or result is to make us either angry or afraid. These are the twin goals of all culture wars propaganda. Anger and fear are our most primitive and instinctive emotions, and they are the surest route (along with sentimentality) to our checkbooks. Neither leads us to love our neighbor, or God either, for that matter. We are eager to cite Jesus' righteous anger in cleansing the temple, but the combination of righteousness and anger is much more problematic in us than it is in him. We would do well to tape these verses from James on our foreheads: "Be quick to listen, slow to speak, and slow to get angry. Human anger does not produce the righteousness God desires" (1:19-20).

Second, we should listen to the stories of those who oppose us. Everyone has a story to tell, and the surest way to conflict is not to allow people to tell their story. A source of frustration for conservative Christians is the feeling that their story has been silenced in the public square, supposedly in the name of allowing other voices to be heard, but not infrequently out of secular hostility to anything religious.

If we want the right to tell our story, however, we must be willing, even anxious, to hear the stories of others. Christians have known what it's like to be the ones not tolerated—throughout history and in some places in the present. It should sensitize us to those who are the object of intolerance today—even to those whose behavior we feel bound not to tolerate ourselves. The people of Israel were often told to remember that they had once been slaves and therefore to treat the stranger fairly. We should do the same by listening to those with whom we are in conflict.

And we should listen compassionately, with a bias toward finding common ground, rather than listening for weakness we can attack. This common ground is not the flaccid "everybody is right" of relativism. The goal is not niceness or pseudo-unanimity but a core set of values and rights that can be affirmed together even as we continue to speak the truth as we understand it.

This won't happen with demonizing, fund-raising rhetoric that only wars against that truth we try to speak.

Tolerance is not a high virtue, but its healthy form is a necessary minimum in the absence of a community of shalom and loving-kindness. It is toward such a community that we all must work, even in the midst of a secular culture. The concept of shalom allows me to state my own guiding principle when it comes to tolerance: Affirm and celebrate anything that contributes to shalom. Tolerate anything that is neutral with regard to shalom. Do not tolerate anything that destroys shalom, unless that intolerance would itself do more harm to shalom than tolerance would.

> **Tolerance is not a high virtue, but its healthy form is a necessary minimum in the absence of a community of shalom and loving-kindness.**

This is not a cure-all principle. It does not tell me exactly what to do in every situation. But it helps me get closer to the mind of God, the One who wishes shalom for his entire creation.

This longer statement of principle can be stated more succinctly: "I wish to be as tolerant as love requires and as truth allows." (In some cases one might substitute the word compassion for love.) Or, to repeat a principle suggested earlier, "I wish to be as tolerant as God is, but not more so."

Do what Jesus would do. Resist appeals to anger and fear. Listen. Work for shalom. Speak the truth in love. If we can make these more than slogans in our lives, we won't have to worry about whether we are tolerant.

I wish to be as tolerant as love requires and as truth allows."

Conclusion

Many on one side of the cultural divide disparage the very concept of sin and traditional morality. Personal choice is all. Many on the other side will declare anyone who talks about common ground a traitor or apostate or, at the least, soft on sin. They will point to the "be ye separate" verses in the Bible and ask how you can share common ground with the devil.

But these are only the loudest voices; they are not the only voices. And they are not, I believe, the voice of God. We have always struggled as fallen beings to understand and live out the implications of the "thou shalt not's" and the "blessed are's" of the Bible. Clearly there are things we ought and ought not to do. And there is no reason to apologize for asserting that to a tone-deaf world.

But it is also clear that the bedrock of all biblical morality is God's love. That love is not incompatible with judgment, but it is incompatible with our not properly valuing all that God has created, including those who offend us.

Must Christians be tolerant? Not really. Certainly not as our society defines the term. God is the standard. Our knowledge of the mind of God on these things is significant—he has revealed much—but it is not complete—he has also concealed much.

What we know for certain is that we must be loving, and that is a far greater challenge than being tolerant, with far greater dangers and rewards.

What we know for certain is that we must be loving, and that is a far greater challenge than being tolerant, with far greater dangers and rewards. Our calling is not to be popular but to be witnesses to the truth to a society that profoundly doubts there is any such thing and is disgusted by anyone suggesting he or she knows what the truth might be.

We must avoid the twin errors of arrogant, authoritarian condemnation on the one hand and relativistic moral paralysis on the other. Between these lies a third possibility: loving faithfulness. We are called to live the gospel as well as to proclaim it. Jesus has provided us the model: Neither do I condemn you. Go and sin no more.

Discussion Questions

CHAPTER 1

1. Have you or anyone in your family experienced intolerance? Have you ever been perceived as being intolerant? What were the circumstances and what, if anything, was the outcome?
2. What is the difference between "putting up with the objectionable" and "affirming the diverse"?
3. What does the following statement mean to you: "God does not call us to be tolerant, he calls us to love"? How would you explain it to a child or young person?
4. "Human beings, in small numbers and large, have always had trouble living at peace with each other." What are some instances that bear this out in biblical history? in secular history? in your family history?
5. How did the rise of empires necessitate a change in the view of tolerance? How did this view affect the early Christian church?
6. For a thousand years, the church and the state ruled Western society together. Why was religious tolerance not a great issue during this time? What changed to make it more important?

7. Define *toleration*. Why was it necessary? How did the European religious wars in the sixteenth and seventeenth centuries influence today's secular view of religion?

8. How does that secular view of religion affect the church and you today? What is your opinion about keeping religion in the private sphere?

9. What are some of the accusations leveled against Christians when they attempt to speak up for their moral values?

10. What would the reaction be in your workplace, school, or neighborhood if you spoke up for your religious beliefs and moral values? What have been your personal experiences in this regard?

CHAPTER 2

1. What is *your* definition of "tolerance" and "intolerance"? How would you explain these terms to a ten-year-old?

2. As defined in this chapter, when are people not truly tolerant even though they claim to be?

3. What are some of the behaviors and ideas that are often confused with tolerance? Name some of the things in your life that fall to the right or left of tolerance on the continuum.

4. Intolerance is often equated with prejudice, bigotry, and judgmentalism. How do these three attitudes/behaviors differ from each other? Why

must we look at real-life situations to evaluate tolerance and intolerance?

5. Some say they "hate the sin but love the sinner." Is this possible? Is it common? Give examples where you have seen this work and not work.

6. Is tolerating evil the same as doing evil? Why or why not? Do you agree that there can be *degrees* of tolerance? How do you know when to tolerate something you disagree with and when to fight actively against it?

7. Make two lists—one of objectionable things to be tolerated and one of things never to be tolerated. Compare your list with the lists of others.

8. Define *relativism* and *pluralism*. Where do you see either of these at work in your everyday experience?

9. Has anyone ever responded to you with, "Who are you to say?" What did you answer? What could you have said?

10. Give a brief description of a healthy notion of tolerance. Of a diseased notion of tolerance. Cite examples of each in your experience.

CHAPTER 3

1. Why is the issue of tolerance often a cause of heated debate and confusion in today's culture wars? Do you agree or disagree with the author's analysis? Why?

2. Have you ever heard anyone use any of these common slogans? What are some others?

3. What does the slogan "Who are you to say?" mean to you? Why is it misguided?

4. Has anyone ever accused you of "forcing your values" on them? Have you ever felt others were trying to force their values on you? How did you react in each case?

5. Are there any circumstances where people *should* "force their values" on others? What is the difference between a legitimate attempt to influence and "forcing one's values" on others?

6. "The concept of tolerance has been misused and redefined in the current cultural debate to make even the attempt to persuade an act of intolerance." What are some of the redefinitions of words and acts that make those accused of intolerance "look stupid or heartless or both"?

7. How can associating one cause with a different popular cause (past or present) be a useful strategy in the culture wars?

8. Are Christians unfairly accused of intolerance? Discuss examples of healthy and unhealthy Christian intolerance.

9. Discuss the account of Mary Sykes Wylie and her day among the Christians. If you could talk with her, how would you respond to her assertions and accusations?

10. Do you think there is a moral community left in this relativistic world? How do compassion and truth work together in a moral community?

CHAPTER 4

1. Do you think God is tolerant? intolerant? Give examples.

2. Explain how the concept of tolerance works in the three different relationships discussed in this chapter.

3. What are some of the characteristics of God depicted in his relationship to humanity? How are these shown in Exodus 34:6-7? Explain the terms "cheap grace" and "lightning-bolt destroyer."

4. Define *shalom* in your own words. List some of the biblical meanings for the word. What is the essence of shalom?

5. Why is it so important for Christians to achieve shalom among themselves? What is the difference between the secular notion of tolerance and the biblical concept of shalom?

6. Based on Paul's writings, how might he react to today's emphasis on radical individualism? What attitudes and actions does Paul commend for believers so they can live in peace? (See Romans 12 and Colossians 3.)

7. In the biblical sense of peace as explained by Paul, "putting up with" something is not enough. What

is necessary to achieve true peace (shalom)? Why is it so difficult?

8. How does the message of John 3:16 define God's relationship with the people who are not Christians? How can you use that message to define your own relationship to unbelievers?

9. What can we learn about tolerance from Christ's story of the Good Samaritan? What does it *not* tell us? What about the story of Zacchaeus? Of the woman caught in adultery?

10. Read the last paragraph of this chapter. Discuss what it says about God's tolerance and our own.

CHAPTER 5

1. Discuss the Aleksandr Solzhenitsyn quotation from *The Gulag Achipelago*. How does that relate to tolerance and intolerance in religion and in the world generally? Do you agree or disagree with Solzhenitsyn's statement?

2. Which of the "thinking" questions listed seem most relevant to your own experience? Which may be most difficult to put into practice?

3. Which of the "speaking and acting" questions listed seem most relevant to your own experience? Which may be most difficult to put into practice?

4. Do the dual questions of "What would Jesus do and how would he do it?" offer a realistic

guideline for living? How can we make them more than slogans?

5. Why is it so difficult for Christians to be like Christ?

6. Read James 1:19-20. How can this Bible passage be a guide in your attempt to "be like Christ"? Why is listening to others so essential to being tolerant and establishing shalom?

7. Read the last paragraphs of the Guidelines and Principles section. Discuss how you could put these into practice in your life—or how you already do.

8. What is the bedrock of all biblical morality? How is it relevant to the culture wars and the question of tolerance?

9. Do you agree that Christians are not required to be tolerant? How would you state for yourself the proper goal for Christians in these matters?

10. How has this book changed or enhanced your understanding of the issue of tolerance? How might it affect how you think and act?

Notes

INTRODUCTION

1. See discussion in Robert Weissburg, *Political Tolerance: Balancing Community and Diversity* (Thousand Oaks, Calif.: Sage Press, 1998), 15.

CHAPTER 1

1. J. Budziszewski, *True Tolerance: Liberalism and the Necessity of Judgment* (New Brunswick, N.J.: Transaction Publishers, 1992), 289.

CHAPTER 2

1. One could argue that indifference should be at the middle of the continuum with tolerance being a step toward rejection. I would suggest, however, that indifference has more of rejection in it than celebration, not even considering something worthy of consideration. Tolerance, having elements both of rejection and acceptance, is a more genuine midpoint on the continuum.

   My colleague Daniel Ritchie suggests an even further point on the continuum is the *requiring* of a certain behavior or the *mandated* acceptance of an idea.

2. David Heyd, ed., *Toleration: An Elusive Virtue* (Princeton: Princeton University Press, 1996), 4.

3. J. Budziszewski, "A War of Words," *Boundless,* 30 September 1998, <www.boundless.org>.

4. F. C. S. Schiller, quoted in Jay Newman, *Foundations of Religious Tolerance* (Toronto: University of Toronto Press, 1982), 57.

5. Quoted in Robert Jewett, *Christian Tolerance: Paul's Message to the Modern Church* (Philadelphia: Westminster Press, 1982), 92.

6. "The Commitment of the Self and the Freedom of the Mind," in Reinhold Niebuhr et al., *Religion and Freedom of Thought* (New York: Doubleday, 1954), 56.

CHAPTER 3

1. Robert Weissberg, "The Abduction of Tolerance," *Society* (November/December 1998): 13.

2. Andrei Codrescu, commentary on *All Things Considered,* National Public Radio, 19 December 1995.

3. Noel Holston, "KTCA Program Provides a Poignant, Powerful Look at Life of Gays, Lesbians," *Minneapolis Star-Tribune,* 20 September 1993, Variety section.

4. Ira Glasser, executive director, ACLU fund-raising letter, n.d.

5. Those interested in such a survey can see Josh McDowell, *The New Tolerance: How a Cultural Movement Threatens to Destroy You, Your Faith, and Your Children* (Wheaton, Ill.: Tyndale House, 1998).

6. Mary Sykes Wylie, "Soul Therapy," *Family Therapy Networker* (January/February 2000).

Recommended Reading

Budziszewski, J. *True Tolerance: Liberalism and the Necessity of Judgment*. New Brunswick, N.J.: Transaction Publishers, 1992.

Gaede, Stan. *When Tolerance Is No Virtue: Political Correctness, Multiculturalism and the Future of Truth and Justice*. Downers Grove, Ill.: InterVarsity Press, 1993.

Heyd, David, ed. *Toleration: An Elusive Virtue*. Princeton: Princeton University Press, 1996.

Jewett, Robert. *Christian Tolerance: Paul's Message to the Modern Church*. Philadelphia: Westminster Press, 1982.

Midgley, Mary. *Can't We Make Moral Judgments?* New York: St. Martin's Press, 1991.

Newman, Jay. *Foundations of Religious Tolerance*. Toronto: University of Toronto Press, 1982.

Tinder, Glenn. *Tolerance: Toward a New Civility*. Amherst: University of Massachusetts Press, 1976.

Weissberg, Robert. *Political Tolerance: Balancing Community and Diversity*. Thousand Oaks, Calif.: Sage Press, 1998.

Topical Index

authoritarianism 63, 75–76
bigotry 22–23, 71–72
Christianity 5, 10–11, 57–58, 69–70
    early views on toleration 13–14, 17
    conservatives 62–66, 68–71, 77, 107
    persecution 11–12, 28–29
church 9, 11–12, 62–63, 86, 93, 97–98, 111–112
coercion 58
community 9, 30, 32, 75–76, 88–93, 95, 99
    believing 77
    faith 83
    shalom and 85–87, 118
contemporary values 36–37
    diversity 10, 12, 37
    individualism 37, 87
    self-actualization 37
definitions [control of debate] 47
discernment 23–24, 35–36
discrimination 23–24
God
    faithfulness 79
    forgiveness 96
    gracious 79
    intolerant 7
    judgment 79
    love 7, 79, 94–96
    merciful 79
    tolerant 78, 96
homosexuality 26, 107
intolerance 20–26
    definition 20

    moral conservatives 2
    religious values 3
judgment 22–24, 52
    individual judgment 30–31, 36
    judgmentalism 51, 102
moral community 75–76
moral passivity 20, 102
neighbor 99–102, 105
pluralism 38
prejudice 22–23
relativism 38
repentance 82, 99
shalom 83–87, 90–93
    definition 83–84
sin 78, 81, 119
slogans 50–55
tolerance
    among believers 83–93
    arguments against 32
    between believers and
      world 94–108
    changing the definition 47–50
    defenses of 28–32
    definition 4–5, 18–24
    degrees of 18–27
    of error 31
    healthy and unhealthy 20, 42–46
    God and humanity 77–82
    principles of 114–119
    versus acceptance, affirmation 21
    versus bigotry, prejudice 22–23
    versus impotence 19
    versus indifference 19
toleration 13–14
truth 7

About the Author

Daniel Taylor teaches at Bethel College (Minnesota) and is the author of various books, including *The Myth of Certainty* and *Tell Me a Story: The Life-Shaping Power of Our Stories*. He is cofounder of The Legacy Center and a contributing editor to *Books and Culture*. Dr. Taylor serves as the general editor of the Vital Questions series.

The Vital Questions Series

CLEAR THINKING FOR FAITHFUL LIVING

□ □

The Vital Questions Series investigates key issues that make a practical difference in how Christians think and act. Each book's goal is to provide a substantial, accessible discussion of issues about which Christians need to know more.

Look for the Vital Questions series wherever fine books are sold:

Is God Intolerant?
by Daniel Taylor

In contemporary culture, Christians have been called intolerant for standing up for what is right, for witnessing to other people about Jesus, and for stating that Jesus is the only way to God. In this volume, Dan Taylor, professor at Bethel College, explores the concept of tolerance. With depth and precision, he explains what true tolerance is and whether God wants Christians to be tolerant.

How *Shall* We Worship?
by Marva J. Dawn

If your church is like most churches, you have debated the value of various types of worship styles in your service—traditional versus contemporary, hymns versus praise songs. It's too easy for people to take sides in the worship wars. Marva Dawn will help you understand why there are so many disagreements in the church about worship. You'll never view worship the same after reading this book.

Does God Need Our Help?
by John F. Kilner and C. Ben Mitchell

Cloning. Assisted suicide. Stem cell research. The advance of biotechnology today is breathtaking. But do we know where all of this is leading us? John F. Kilner and C. Ben Mitchell will lead you on a fascinating journey, explaining the cutting-edge advances in biotechnology. This book will help you formulate an informed and thoroughly Christian perspective on everything from assisted suicide to infertility treatments, from cloning to stem cell research.